DATE DUE

MAY 1 4 1975		
OCT 1 8		
JAN 9		
APR 18		
SEP 25		
N 4 85		
MAR 20 '85		
MAR 1 1 1997		
FAC 97		
NO 02 '00		
MR 31 '04		

GAYLORD   PRINTED IN U.S.A.

Good Housekeeping's
COOKIE-JAR COOKBOOK

By the
Food Editors
of
Good
Housekeeping
Magazine

ILLUSTRATIONS BY
KINUKO CRAFT

PHOTOGRAPHS BY
JAMES VILES

Published by
Consolidated Book Publishers
1727 South Indiana Avenue, Chicago, Illinois 60616

Contents

Nothing makes a kitchen more popular than a well-stocked cookie jar. Not only are the children happier—for it seems that cookies were made especially for them—but the homemaker whose cookie jar is always well filled is never at a loss for what to serve *Cookie-Jar Cookbook* the unexpected guest. § Because almost all cookies are easy to make and will keep for some time, they are the ideal treat for the busy homemaker's hungry family. Fond memories of home often center around the cookies-and-milk snacks that your children and their friends shared at the kitchen table after school. Even the man of the house expects at least seconds when the tempting aroma of baking cookies fills the kitchen air. § We know that if you form the habit of having your own home-baked cookies always on hand, you will wonder how you ever managed without them. That is why we have collected these recipes for you. We urge you to try each and every one, and see for yourself how popular your kitchen becomes. And we think you will treasure the compliments that are headed your way.

HELPS FOR THE COOKIE MAKER

1. *For the soft shortening* called for in some of our cookie recipes, use any shortening that is in condition to be creamed easily. If necessary, let it stand at room temperature until soft.
2. *Most of our cookie recipes were tested using regular all-purpose flour.* Do not substitute unless recipe so directs, or unless an alternate flour suggestion is given.
3. *With an electric mixer* (portable or on a stand), you can whisk a batch of cookies together in no time. Just follow our recipes, using medium speed for mixing shortening, sugar, etc., and low speed for dry ingredients, unless otherwise directed.
4. *If you are mixing with a spoon,* use a wooden one with a comfortable long handle so you can mix, stir, and beat effectively.
5. *For evenly baked cookies,* use cookie sheets about 2 inches narrower and shorter than your oven, to allow space around edges for heat circulation. If you bake one sheet at a time, place oven rack in center of oven; if two sheets, place racks so they divide oven in thirds.
6. *If cookie sheet is to be greased,* do it lightly. Also, you will avoid hard-to-wash brown patches if you grease or oil only the spots where dough is to drop, allowing space for spreading.
7. *If you need extra cookie sheets,* inverted baking pans may be used. Or cut a piece of foil to fit your one and only cookie sheet. While cookie sheet of cookies bakes, drop more dough onto foil; then place foil on cookie sheet as it comes from the oven and is emptied.
8. *No danger of overbaking cookies* if you use a timer clock to warn you when baking time is up. Then, with a broad spatula, immediately slip baked cookies onto one or more wire racks to cool. Never overlap cookies, or place on top of one another until they are cool.

STORING COOKIES

Soft Cookies: Keep in container with tight-fitting cover. Bar-type cookies may be stored right in baking pan, tightly covered. If the cookies tend to dry out, add a piece of apple, orange, or bread, replacing it often.

Crisp Cookies: Keep in container with loose-fitting cover. If they soften, heat in 300°F. oven about 5 minutes before serving.

TO FREEZE COOKIES

Kinds to Freeze: Molded or cookie-press (Shape-and-Bake), drop, refrigerator (Slice-and-Bake), bar, and roll-and-cut cookies.

Cookie Dough: Form refrigerator-cookie dough into a roll or a bar; then wrap in foil, saran, cellophane, or any suitable sheet wrapping. Pack other cookie doughs in freezer containers.

Baked Cookies: Make and bake as usual; then cut if necessary; cool thoroughly. Arrange on cardboard covered with wax paper or foil; then place in plastic bags. Or pack gently in any freezing bag, box, or container of convenient size. Use a sturdy container for fragile cookies —metal or plastic box, or coffee can. Cushion cookies with crumpled foil or wax paper.

TO USE FROZEN COOKIES

Thaw refrigerator-cookie dough in refrigerator about 1 hour, or until it slices easily. Bake as usual. Thaw any other kind of cookie dough until it can be handled easily; prepare and bake as usual. Thaw baked cookies, unwrapped, about 15 minutes at room temperature.

Drop-and-Bake Cookies

Drop cookies are made from a soft dough which is just stiff enough to be pushed from the spoon. This dough will shape itself while it bakes; therefore, the shape of the cookies will be somewhat irregular. Space the cookies 2 to 3 inches apart on the cookie sheets to allow for spreading.

ALMOND MACAROON CAKES

2 egg whites	1¾ cups ground blanched
¾ cup granulated sugar	almonds
	Whole blanched almonds

A few days ahead:
1. Beat egg whites until they hold soft peaks; then gradually add 6 tablespoons sugar while beating egg whites until stiff.
2. Blend ground almonds with 6 tablespoons sugar; fold carefully into beaten egg whites.
3. Place, by tablespoonfuls, in oval mounds, on greased wax paper on cookie sheets. Top each cake with a blanched almond. Let dry overnight at room temperature.
Next day:
1. Start heating oven to 400°F.
2. Bake cakes 10 to 15 minutes, or until bottoms are light brown and inside still moist.
3. Lift cakes, still on wax paper, from cookie sheets to wet towel; let stand a few minutes until they can easily be removed and transferred to a wire rack to cool. Makes about 18.

ALMOND ROLL COOKIES

⅔ cup canned blanched almonds, finely ground	2 tablespoons milk
½ cup butter or margarine	1 tablespoon regular all-purpose flour
½ cup granulated sugar	Sifted confectioners' sugar

Early on day:
1. Start heating oven to 350°F.
2. In large skillet, combine almonds, butter, granulated sugar, milk, and flour; heat, stirring constantly, over low heat, until butter is melted and mixture is mushy.
3. Drop, by heaping teaspoonfuls, 3 inches apart, onto two well greased and floured cookie sheets.
4. Bake, 1 sheet at a time, 5 or 6 minutes, or until golden; then remove, one at a time, from cookie sheet and quickly roll up around handle of wooden spoon; cool on wire racks.
5. To serve, dust lightly with confectioners' sugar. Makes about 30.

NEW-LOOK ALMOND ROLLS (Pictured on page 5): Prepare batter as above, but drop by level tablespoonfuls, only four to a cookie sheet, at least 3 inches apart. Bake as above. Let cool on cookie sheet a minute or two; then, with wide spatula, remove each cookie, turn over and roll as above. Cool; then fill. (Let cookie sheet cool before using again.)

FILLING: Whip 1 cup heavy cream with ½ teaspoon vanilla extract; spoon into pastry bag with pastry tube number 1. Use to fill each cookie roll. Then garnish with strawberries as pictured.

To vary: Dip one end of each cookie roll in semisweet-chocolate pieces that have been melted over hot, *not boiling*, water. Makes 14 large cookies.

ALMOND WINE BISCUITS

1 cup sifted regular all-purpose flour	½ teaspoon grated lemon peel
⅛ teaspoon salt	½ cup coarsely-ground almonds
½ cup soft shortening	¼ cup sherry
⅓ cup granulated sugar	⅓ cup coarsely-ground almonds
2 egg yolks	
¼ teaspoon anise extract	

1. Start heating oven to 400°F.
2. Sift flour with salt.
3. Mix, until creamy, shortening, sugar, and egg yolks. Add anise, lemon peel, and ½ cup almonds; mix. Beat in sherry alternately with flour mixture, mixing well.
4. Drop, by tablespoonfuls, onto ⅓ cup almonds; toss well to coat with nuts.
5. Place, 1 inch apart, on greased cookie sheet; shape with spoon into 1½-inch rounds, about ½ inch thick.
6. Bake 12 to 15 minutes, or until golden. Makes 1 dozen.

ANISE DROPS

3 eggs, unbeaten	1 teaspoon double-acting baking powder
1 cup granulated sugar, sifted	½ teaspoon vanilla extract
1¾ cups sifted regular all-purpose flour	1½ tablespoons anise seeds

Day before:
1. In large bowl, with mixer at medium speed, beat

4

eggs until light, gradually adding sugar. Then continue beating 10 minutes.

2. Sift flour with baking powder. Add with vanilla to egg mixture, beating at low speed until well blended. Stir in anise seeds.

3. Drop, by heaping teaspoonfuls, onto greased cookie sheets. Let stand, uncovered, overnight at room temperature.

Next day:

1. Start heating oven to 350°F.

2. Bake cookies 8 to 10 minutes, or until pale beige. Store in tightly covered container; they keep indefinitely. To hasten softening, store with a piece of apple. Makes about 3 dozen.

GLAZED FRESH-APPLE COOKIES

2 cups sifted regular all-purpose flour	½ teaspoon nutmeg
1 teaspoon baking soda	1 egg, unbeaten
½ cup soft shortening	1 cup chopped nuts
1⅓ cups brown sugar, packed	1 cup finely-chopped, unpared apple
½ teaspoon salt	1 cup dark or light raisins, chopped
1 teaspoon cinnamon	¼ cup apple juice or milk
1 teaspoon ground cloves	Vanilla Glaze, below

1. Start heating oven to 400°F.

2. Sift flour with baking soda.

3. Mix together shortening, brown sugar, salt, cinnamon, cloves, nutmeg, and egg until well blended. Stir in half of flour mixture, then nuts, apple, and raisins. Blend in apple juice, then remaining flour mixture, mixing well.

4. Drop, by rounded tablespoonfuls, 2 inches apart, onto greased cookie sheets.

5. Bake 11 to 14 minutes, or until done. While cookies are still hot, spread thinly with Vanilla Glaze. Makes 3½ dozen.

VANILLA GLAZE: In small bowl, blend 1½ cups sifted confectioners' sugar with 1 tablespoon soft butter or margarine, ¼ teaspoon vanilla extract, ⅛ teaspoon salt, and 2½ tablespoons light cream.

CHOCOLATE BRAZIL-NUT COOKIES

½ cup soft butter or margarine	2 squares semisweet chocolate, melted
¼ teaspoon salt	¾ cup sifted regular all-purpose flour
1 cup granulated sugar	½ cup finely-chopped Brazil nuts
1 egg, unbeaten	
1 teaspoon vanilla extract	

1. Start heating oven to 325°F.

2. In medium bowl, with mixer at medium speed, cream butter with salt until light and fluffy, gradually adding sugar. Add egg; beat well.

3. Blend in vanilla and chocolate. Mix in flour, then nuts, until well blended.

4. Drop, by level tablespoonfuls, 2 inches apart, onto greased cookie sheets. Stamp lightly with a flat-bottomed glass, covered with a damp cloth. If desired, sprinkle a few Brazil-nut slivers over the top of each cookie.

5. Bake about 15 minutes, or until done. Cool. Makes 3 dozen.

FROSTED CHOCOLATE-NUT DROPS

1¼ cups sifted regular all-purpose flour	1 teaspoon vanilla extract
¼ teaspoon baking soda	½ teaspoon salt
½ cup soft shortening	½ cup buttermilk or 7 tablespoons milk plus 2 teaspoons vinegar
1 cup brown sugar, firmly packed	1 cup walnuts, coarsely chopped
1 egg, unbeaten	Creamy Frosting, below
2 squares unsweetened chocolate, melted	

1. Start heating oven to 350°F.

2. Sift flour with baking soda.

3. In large bowl, with mixer at medium speed, mix shortening, brown sugar, egg, chocolate, vanilla, and salt until well blended. Stir in flour mixture, then blend in buttermilk. Stir in nuts.

4. Drop, by level tablespoonfuls, 2 inches apart, onto greased cookie sheets.

5. Bake 12 to 15 minutes, or until top springs back when lightly touched. Cool; then frost with Creamy Frosting. Makes 3 dozen.

CREAMY FROSTING: With mixer at medium speed (or with spoon), thoroughly mix ⅓ cup soft butter, margarine, or shortening with ⅛ teaspoon salt and 1 cup sifted confectioners' sugar until light and fluffy. Add about 2 cups sifted confectioners' sugar alternately with 4 to 5 tablespoons hot light cream, beating until very smooth and of spreading consistency; add 1½ teaspoons vanilla extract.

CHOCOLATE-TIPPED ACCORDIAN STRIPS
(Pictured on page 54)

3 eggs, unbeaten	Butter or margarine, melted
¾ cup granulated sugar	No-Melt Chocolate Glaze, page 6
1⅓ cups sifted cake flour	
1 tablespoon grated lemon peel	

Make anytime up to 3 days ahead:

1. Tear off 27 inches of heavy-duty foil; fold in half lengthwise; then fold, crosswise, into 1-inch pleats; lay on ungreased cookie sheet. Pull these accordian pleats apart a bit.

2. Start heating oven to 350°F.

3. In large bowl, with mixer at medium speed, beat

New-Look Almond Rolls

eggs with sugar until light and fluffy; gradually beat in flour and lemon peel. Mix well.

4. Brush accordian pleats slightly with melted butter; drop a rounded tablespoonful of cookie dough in center of each (dough will spread in baking).

5. Bake 15 to 20 minutes.

6. Let cool 10 minutes; then remove from foil to wire racks. Scrape all crumbs from foil pleats; turn on other side and repeat with rest of dough.

7. When cookies are cool, dip or spread both ends of each cookie, about 1½ to 2 inches in, with No-Melt Chocolate Glaze. Place on wire racks, with wax paper below, to dry. Store in cakebox. Makes 2 dozen.

NO-MELT CHOCOLATE GLAZE: In small saucepan melt 2 tablespoons butter or margarine; stir in 2 envelopes (2 ounces) no-melt unsweetened chocolate; then with spoon, beat in 1 cup sifted confectioners' sugar and ¼ cup hot water until smooth.

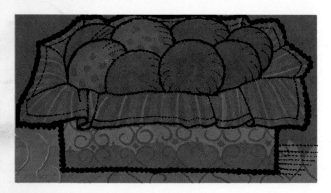

CHOCOLATE VENETIANS
(Pictured on page 12)

1 cup granulated sugar	⅛ teaspoon nutmeg
2 eggs, unbeaten	1 cup finely-chopped
2 tablespoons sifted regular	blanched almonds
all-purpose flour	¼ cup chopped candied
⅛ teaspoon double-acting	orange peel
baking powder	1 teaspoon grated lemon
¼ teaspoon salt	peel
¼ teaspoon cinnamon	Chocolate Brandy Glaze,
⅛ teaspoon ground cloves	below

Make a few days ahead:

1. Start heating oven to 400°F.

2. In large bowl, with mixer at medium speed, blend sugar with eggs well.

3. Gradually beat in flour, baking powder, salt, cinnamon, cloves, and nutmeg; stir in nuts, orange peel, and lemon peel.

4. Drop, by teaspoonfuls, 2 inches apart, onto foil-lined cookie sheets.

5. Bake 7 minutes.

6. Cool cookies 7 minutes; then peel off foil.

7. Meanwhile, make Chocolate Brandy Glaze. Turn cookies upside down, then frost with glaze. Makes about 5½ dozen.

CHOCOLATE BRANDY GLAZE: Melt 1 6-ounce package (1 cup) semisweet-chocolate pieces and 2 tablespoons butter or margarine over hot, *not boiling*, water. Remove from heat; blend in ¼ cup brandy.

CHOCOLATE-JUBILEE JUMBLES

2¾ cups sifted regular all-purpose flour	2 eggs, unbeaten
½ teaspoon baking soda	1 cup undiluted evaporated milk
1 teaspoon salt	1 teaspoon vanilla extract
½ cup soft shortening	1 cup broken walnut meats
1 cup brown sugar, packed	Burnt Butter Glaze, below
½ cup granulated sugar	

1. Sift flour with baking soda and salt.

2. In large bowl, with mixer at medium speed (or with spoon), mix shortening with sugars and eggs until light and fluffy; then stir in milk and vanilla.

3. With spoon, mix in flour mixture, then walnuts;* refrigerate about 1 hour.

4. Meanwhile, make Burnt Butter Glaze.

5. Start heating oven to 375°F.

6. When cookie mixture is chilled, drop, by rounded tablespoonfuls, 2 inches apart, onto greased cookie sheets.

7. Bake 10 to 12 minutes, or until golden.

8. While cookies are still warm, frost with Burnt Butter Glaze. Makes 3½ to 4 dozen.

*1 cup flaked coconut, finely cut pitted dates, or seedless raisins may be added here.

BURNT BUTTER GLAZE: In saucepan, heat 2 tablespoons butter or margarine until golden brown. Beat in 2 cups sifted confectioners' sugar and ¼ cup undiluted evaporated milk until smooth; fold in 1 cup semisweet-chocolate pieces.

CANDY COOKIES
(Pictured on page 12)

½ cup soft shortening	½ teaspoon salt
½ cup brown sugar, packed	½ teaspoon baking soda
¼ cup granulated sugar	¾ cup packaged chocolate-covered raisins
1 egg, unbeaten	¼ cup coarsely-chopped walnuts
½ teaspoon vanilla extract	
1 cup plus 2 tablespoons sifted regular all-purpose flour	

Make a few days ahead:

1. Start heating oven to 375°F.

2. In large bowl, with mixer at medium speed, beat shortening with brown sugar and granulated sugar until light and fluffy.

3. Beat in egg and vanilla.

4. Sift flour with salt and baking soda. At low speed, beat flour mixture into shortening-sugar mixture until batter is smooth. Then fold in raisins and walnuts.

5. Drop, by teaspoonfuls, onto greased cookie sheets.

6. Bake 10 to 12 minutes, or until they are lightly browned. Remove to wire rack to cool. Makes 2½ to 3 dozen.

CRUNCHY COOKIES
(Pictured on page 8)

½ cup soft shortening
½ cup granulated sugar
½ cup liquid honey
1 egg, unbeaten
1½ cups sifted regular all-
  purpose flour
½ teaspoon baking soda
1 teaspoon salt

1 teaspoon cinnamon
¼ cup milk
½ cup dark or light raisins
½ cup coarsely-chopped
  walnuts
4 shredded-wheat biscuits,
  crumbled

1. Start heating oven to 375°F.

2. In large bowl, with mixer at medium speed, beat shortening with sugar, honey, and egg until well blended.

3. Meanwhile, sift flour with baking soda, salt, and cinnamon. Beat flour mixture into sugar mixture alternately with milk.

4. Stir in raisins, walnuts, and shredded wheat crumbs.

5. Drop dough, by heaping teaspoonfuls, onto greased cookie sheets.

6. Bake 12 to 15 minutes, or until done.

7. Cool on wire racks. Store in tightly covered container. Makes 45.

MARBLE CURLS
(Pictured on page 47)

1 recipe dough for
  Chocolate-Tipped
  Accordian Strips, page 4

2 teaspoons cocoa

Make up to a week ahead:

1. Start heating oven to 350°F.

2. Make dough as directed. For marble effect, mix ⅓ cup of dough with cocoa.

3. Spoon 1 teaspoonful of regular dough onto greased cookie sheet in strip about 5 inches by 1 inch. Repeat, having 6 strips on sheet. Then, with small spoon, drizzle some of cocoa mixture very lightly on each strip.

4. Bake cookies 4 to 8 minutes, or until edges are light golden.

5. Immediately, with spatula, remove each strip from cookie sheet and twist over handle of wooden spoon. Should strips harden, return to oven to soften. Repeat with rest of dough. Store in tightly covered container. Makes about 3 dozen.

GOLDEN COCONUT MOUNDS

2 eggs, unbeaten
1 cup granulated sugar
3 3½-ounce packages flaked
  coconut (3 cups)

¼ cup sifted regular all-
  purpose flour

Make several days ahead, if desired:

1. Start heating oven to 350°F.

2. In large bowl, with mixer at high speed, beat eggs with sugar *just until well blended*—about 1 minute; then fold in coconut and flour all at once.

3. Drop, about 2 tablespoonfuls at a time, 2 inches apart, onto two lightly-greased cookie sheets. Shape into peaked mounds.

4. Bake 10 to 18 minutes, or until golden on tops and bottoms. (Cookies will be soft to touch and will firm up when they cool.)

5. Cool on wire racks; then store in tightly covered container until read to serve — flavor develops upon standing. Makes 15.

PECAN KISSES

2 egg whites
2 cups sifted confectioners'
  sugar

1 teaspoon vinegar
1 teaspoon vanilla extract
2 cups pecan halves

1. Start heating oven to 300°F.

2. With mixer at high speed, or hand beater, beat egg whites until stiff but not dry. Gradually beat in confectioners' sugar, vinegar, and vanilla; carefully fold in pecans.

3. Drop, by teaspoonfuls, 2 inches apart, onto greased cookie sheets.

4. Bake 12 to 15 minutes, or until firm. (Cookies should remain light.)

5. Remove from cookie sheets at once; cool. Makes 3½ dozen.

POPCORN MACAROONS
(Pictured on page 12)

2 cups popped popcorn
6 egg whites
¼ teaspoon salt
1 teaspoon cream of tartar
2 cups sifted confectioners'
  sugar

2 teaspoons vanilla extract
2 cups pecan halves,
  finely chopped
About 30 drained glacéed
  cherries (from jar)

Make several days ahead, if desired:

1. Put popped corn through fine food chopper.

2. In large bowl, with mixer at high speed, beat egg whites with salt until foamy. Add cream of tartar and beat until egg whites form soft peaks. Then, with mixer at low speed, gradually beat in confectioners' sugar. Fold in vanilla, popcorn, and pecans.

3. Start heating oven to 275°F.

*Muffin-Pan Crispies, Crunchy Cookies, Quick Macaroons,
Surprise Balls, Chocolate-Sugar Twins, Crescent Meltaways*

4. Using a number 30 ice-cream scoop, or a large serving spoon of 2-tablespoons size, drop cookies, 1 inch apart, onto lightly-greased, paper-covered cookie sheet (refrigerate rest of batter). Top each cookie with a cherry.

5. Bake 1 hour—they will be soft.

6. Remove cookies, on paper, from cookie sheet. Cool cookies on paper while baking rest; then remove cooled ones; store, covered, until ready to serve. Makes 30.

LEMON-PEEL WHEELS
(Pictured on page 54)

1½ cups instant-type flour*	½ cup granulated sugar
1 teaspoon double-acting baking powder	1 teaspoon grated lemon peel
1 teaspoon salt	1 egg, unbeaten
½ cup soft shortening	⅓ cup liquid honey

Make up to a week ahead, if desired:

1. Start heating oven to 350°F.

2. Mix flour with baking powder and salt.

3. In large bowl, with mixer at medium speed, beat shortening with sugar and lemon peel until light and fluffy. Beat in egg and honey; then beat in flour mixture gradually.

4. Drop, by rounded tablespoonfuls, onto greased cookie sheets. With 4-tined fork mark center top of each cookie, first from one side, then from opposite side as pictured.

5. Bake 12 minutes, or until golden at edges.

6. Remove, while hot, to wire racks to cool. Decorate with more grated lemon peel. Makes about 24.
*Do not sift this flour.

GOLDEN MAPLE BUTTER ROLL-UPS
(Pictured on page 54)

½ cup white corn syrup	¼ teaspoon maple flavoring
½ cup brown sugar, packed	¾ cup instant-type flour*
½ cup butter or margarine	½ cup walnuts, chopped

Make up to a week ahead:

1. Start heating oven to 325°F.

2. In medium saucepan heat corn syrup, brown sugar, and butter. Stir in maple flavoring and flour; then add walnuts.

3. Drop, by level teaspoonfuls, 4 inches apart, onto greased cookie sheets.

4. Bake 6 to 7 minutes.

5. Remove from oven; let stand 1 minute. Remove, one at a time, from cookie sheet; quickly roll around handle of wooden spoon. (If cookies get too hard to roll, reheat in oven a minute or two to soften.) Repeat with remaining dough. Cool; refrigerate. Makes 5 dozen.
*Do not sift this flour.

To freeze: Make, bake, and roll cookies as above, then freezer-wrap and freeze up to 2 months. When needed, thaw, unwrapped, at room temperature, about 15 minutes before serving.

BUTTERSCOTCH OAT DROPS

1 cup brown sugar, firmly packed	½ teaspoon baking soda
¾ cup soft butter or margarine	1 6-ounce package butterscotch pieces (1 cup)
2 eggs, unbeaten	1 cup uncooked quick-cooking rolled oats
2 cups instant-type flour*	½ cup walnuts, finely chopped
½ teaspoon salt	

Early on day:

1. Start heating oven to 350°F.

2. In large bowl, with mixer at medium speed, beat brown sugar with butter until creamy; then beat in eggs, one at a time.

3. On wax paper, combine flour, salt, and baking soda; gradually beat into sugar mixture. Then, with spoon, stir in butterscotch pieces, rolled oats, and nuts until well mixed.

4. Drop, by well-rounded teaspoonfuls, 2 inches apart, onto greased cookie sheets.

5. Bake 12 to 14 minutes.

6. Remove with wide spatula to wire rack to cool. Store in tightly covered container. Makes about 57 cookies.
*Do not sift this flour.

To freeze: Make and bake as above, then freezer-wrap and freeze up to 2 months before using. Thaw, unwrapped, at room temperature, about 15 minutes before serving.

MUFFIN-PAN CRISPIES
(Pictured opposite)

½ cup soft butter or margarine	1 teaspoon vanilla extract
⅔ cup light-brown sugar, packed	1½ cups uncooked rolled oats
¼ teaspoon salt	1 tablespoon milk
½ teaspoon double-acting baking powder	¼ cup hot water
	¼ teaspoon cinnamon
	Dash nutmeg

Make 1 hour before serving:

1. Start heating oven to 350°F.

2. In medium bowl, with mixer at medium speed, mix ¼ cup butter or margarine with ⅓ cup light-brown sugar, salt, baking powder, and vanilla extract until mixture is smooth. Stir in rolled oats, then milk; mix until well blended.

3. Into each of 12 ungreased muffin-pan cups, measuring 2 inches across bottom, lightly pile about 1½ tablespoonfuls of rolled-oats mixture; with fork, very gently level off top of each.

4. Bake 15 minutes.

5. Meanwhile, in saucepan, melt ¼ cup butter; stir in ⅓ cup brown sugar, hot water, cinnamon, and nutmeg. Heat about 2 minutes, stirring constantly.

6. At end of 15 minutes baking, remove cookies from oven and spoon about 1½ teaspoons butter-brown sugar sauce over each. Return to oven for 15 minutes.

7. With thin-bladed spatula, *very* carefully loosen edges of each cookie from pan all around, pressing gently toward center. Cool 5 minutes, then gradually remove from pans; finish cooling on paper towels on wire rack. Store in tightly covered container; these cookies keep well. Makes 1 dozen.

ORANGE-OATMEAL COOKIES

2 cups sifted regular all-purpose flour	1 cup soft shortening
2 cups granulated sugar	2 eggs, unbeaten
4 teaspoons double-acting baking powder	4 tablespoons grated orange peel
1 teaspoon salt	2 tablespoons orange juice
1 teaspoon nutmeg	3 cups uncooked quick-cooking rolled oats

1. Start heating oven to 375°F.

2. Into large bowl, sift flour with sugar, baking powder, salt, and nutmeg. Add shortening, eggs, orange peel, and orange juice; mix until well blended. Stir in rolled oats.

3. Drop, by level tablespoonfuls, 2 inches apart, onto greased cookie sheets.

4. Bake 15 minutes, or until done.

5. Remove to wire racks to cool. Makes 4 dozen.

CHOCOLATE-OAT MEDALLIONS

½ cup butter or margarine	¼ cup chopped walnuts
¾ cup granulated sugar	½ teaspoon rum extract
1½ cups uncooked quick-cooking rolled oats	¼ cup finely-chopped semisweet-chocolate pieces
½ cup heavy cream	

Make several days ahead:

1. Start heating oven to 375°F.

2. In small bowl, with mixer at high speed, mix butter with sugar until very light and fluffy; with spoon, fold in rolled oats.

3. Drop, by heaping measuring teaspoonfuls, 3 inches apart, onto greased cookie sheets, making 36 to 40 in all.

4. Bake 8 to 10 minutes, or until golden around edges.

5. Remove from oven; let stand on cookie sheets about 1 minute, or until firm enough to remove to wire racks to cool. Store in tightly covered container.

Just before serving:

1. Whip cream; mix in walnuts, rum extract, and semisweet-chocolate pieces.

2. Spread on cookies and put together sandwich-fashion. Or fill with Chocolate Butter Cream, below. Makes about 1½ dozen.

CHOCOLATE BUTTER CREAM: With mixer at medium speed (or with spoon), thoroughly mix ½ cup soft butter, margarine, or shortening with ⅛ teaspoon salt and 1 cup sifted confectioners' sugar until light and fluffy. Add 2 unbeaten egg yolks and 3 squares melted unsweetened chocolate. Add about 2 cups sifted confectioners' sugar, alternately with about ⅛ to ¼ cup milk or light cream, beating until very smooth and of spreading consistency; add 1½ teaspoons vanilla extract.

SEMISWEET OATMEAL COOKIES

¾ cup sifted regular all-purpose flour	6 tablespoons brown sugar
½ teaspoon baking soda	½ teaspoon vanilla extract
½ teaspoon salt	¼ teaspoon water
½ cup soft butter or margarine	1 egg, unbeaten
6 tablespoons granulated sugar	1 cup uncooked rolled oats
	1 6-ounce package semisweet-chocolate pieces (1 cup)

1. Start heating oven to 375°F.

2. Sift flour with baking soda and salt; set aside.

3. Blend together butter, granulated sugar, brown sugar, vanilla, and water. Beat in egg. Add flour mixture; mix well. Stir in rolled oats and semisweet-chocolate pieces.

4. Drop, by rounded half-teaspoonfuls, onto greased cookie sheets.

5. Bake 10 to 12 minutes.

6. Remove to wire racks to cool. Makes 4 dozen.

SPICED OATMEAL DROPS

2 cups granulated sugar	1 teaspoon ground cloves
1 cup soft shortening	1 teaspoon baking soda
2 eggs, unbeaten	1 teaspoon double-acting baking powder
⅓ cup light molasses	1 cup undiluted evaporated milk
3 cups sifted regular all-purpose flour	3 cups uncooked quick-cooking rolled oats
1 teaspoon salt	
1 teaspoon cinnamon	
1 teaspoon nutmeg	

Make up to 2 weeks ahead:

1. Start heating oven to 350°F.

2. In large bowl, with mixer at medium speed, blend sugar, shortening, eggs, and molasses until light and fluffy.

3. Onto wax paper, sift flour with salt, cinnamon, nutmeg, cloves, baking soda, and baking powder. Beat this mixture, alternately with evaporated milk, into shortening mixture. Then beat in rolled oats.

4. Drop, by tablespoonfuls, onto well-greased cookie sheets.

5. Bake 15 to 18 minutes, or until light brown.
6. Remove from cookie sheets to wire rack to cool. Makes about 120 cookies.

To freeze: Make and bake cookies as above, then freezer-wrap and freeze up to 2 months. To serve, thaw, unwrapped, at room temperature, about 15 minutes.

MOLASSES SNAPS

2 cups sifted regular all- purpose flour	½ cup light-brown sugar, packed
1 teaspoon baking soda	½ cup light molasses
½ cup soft shortening	1 egg, unbeaten
½ teaspoon salt	Cinnamon and granulated
1 teaspoon cinnamon	sugar
1 teaspoon ginger	21 blanched almonds, split

1. Start heating oven to 350°F.
2. Sift flour with baking soda.
3. Mix shortening, salt, cinnamon, ginger, brown sugar, molasses, and egg until well blended; stir in flour mixture.
4. Drop, by level tablespoonfuls, 2 inches apart, onto greased cookie sheets; stamp lightly with flat-bottomed glass, covered with a damp cloth. Sprinkle cookies with a mixture of cinnamon and granulated sugar; then press almond half in center of each.
5. Bake 12 to 15 minutes. Makes about 3½ dozen.

SOFT MOLASSES "JUMBALS"

2¼ cups sifted regular all- purpose flour	½ cup soft shortening
1 teaspoon ginger	½ cup granulated sugar
1 teaspoon cinnamon	½ cup molasses
¼ teaspoon salt	1 egg, unbeaten
2 teaspoons baking soda	6 tablespoons cold water
2 tablespoons hot water	½ cup light or dark raisins or chopped walnuts

Make several days ahead, or early on day:
1. Start heating oven to 400°F.
2. Sift flour with ginger, cinnamon, and salt. Dissolve baking soda in hot water.
3. In large bowl, with mixer at medium speed, blend shortening, sugar, molasses, and egg until *very light and fluffy*. Blend in flour mixture alternately with cold water; then mix in baking soda and all but a few raisins.
4. Drop, by rounded tablespoonfuls, 2 inches apart, onto greased cookie sheet; top with rest of raisins.
5. Bake 12 minutes, or until done.
6. Remove to wire racks to cool. Makes about 2 dozen.

SALTED-PEANUT COOKIES

1½ cups sifted regular all- purpose flour	1¼ cups brown sugar, packed
½ teaspoon double-acting baking powder	1 egg, unbeaten
¾ teaspoon baking soda	¼ cup milk
½ teaspoon salt	1½ cups whole-wheat flakes or bran flakes
½ cup soft butter or margarine	(with or without raisins)
	¾ cup salted peanuts, chopped

1. Start heating oven to 375°F.
2. Sift flour with baking powder, baking soda, and salt.
3. Cream butter until light and fluffy, gradually adding brown sugar. Add egg; beat well. Add flour mixture alternately with milk, mixing well after each addition. Stir in flakes and peanuts.
4. Drop, by level tablespoonfuls, onto greased cookie sheets.
5. Bake 8 minutes, or until done.
6. Remove to wire racks to cool. Makes 4½ dozen.

ORANGE ROCK CAKES

3 cups sifted regular all- purpose flour	½ cup granulated sugar
3 teaspoons double-acting baking powder	2 eggs, unbeaten
	Grated orange peel
½ teaspoon salt	½ cup orange juice
½ cup butter or margarine	Orange Glaze, below

Make a few days ahead:
1. Start heating oven to 400°F.
2. Sift flour with baking powder and salt.
3. In large bowl, with mixer at medium speed, beat butter with sugar until light and fluffy. Beat in eggs, one at a time. Add flour mixture, 3 tablespoons orange peel, and orange juice, beating at low speed until blended.
4. Drop, by tablespoonfuls, in oval shapes, onto greased cookie sheets.
5. Bake 15 to 20 minutes, or until light golden.
6. Remove to wire rack; cool. Dribble Orange Glaze over cooled cakes; then sprinkle with more grated orange peel. Makes about 32.

ORANGE GLAZE: In small bowl blend 1⅓ cups sifted confectioners' sugar with 5 to 6 teaspoons orange juice until smooth.

Our cookie counter is all dressed up for Christmas, but there is no doubt that these delicious cookies will be received with cheers at any time of year. Starting at the top left of the showcase you see Spice-Cookie Lollipops, then next in line are Sugar Shapes, Yum-Yums, and some cherry-topped Popcorn

Cookie Counter

Macaroons. Inside the showcase in the back row there are two-layered Apricot-Walnut Bars, Chocolate Venetians, and cakelike Orange Saucepan Cookies. § Below them: a pile of Cinnamon-Ginger Wafers, Chocolate-Butterscotch Bars, and Candy Cookies (chocolate-coated raisins baked into crunchy rounds). Then come Chocolate Cornflake Clusters, "quickie" cookies that need no baking. § In the bottom row of the showcase you see Scotch Fans, so easy to make, and tasting like the shortest of shortbreads, Gingerbread Boys that could just as easily be gingerbread girls, more Sugar Shapes like the angels on top, Pecan Puffs, a stack of Golden Almond Crisps, Chocolate Crackle-Tops, Brazil-Nut Snowballs, and, finally, Peppermint Fluffs, cookie-wafers topped with peppermint meringue. Which ones will you choose?

ORANGE CRISPIES

1 cup soft shortening	1½ teaspoons orange
½ teaspoon salt	extract
1 cup granulated sugar	1½ cups sifted regular all-
1 egg, unbeaten	purpose flour

1. Start heating oven to 375°F.
2. Cream shortening with salt until light and fluffy, gradually adding sugar. Add egg; beat well. Blend in orange extract, then flour.
3. Drop, by rounded tablespoonfuls, 2 inches apart, onto ungreased cookie sheets.
4. Bake 10 minutes, or until edges are light brown.
5. Let stand 1 or 2 minutes before removing to wire rack to cool. If desired, while cookies are still warm, sprinkle with granulated sugar. Makes 4 dozen.

SUNSHINE PINEAPPLE COOKIES

1 cup butter or margarine	3½ cups sifted regular all-
1½ cups granulated sugar	purpose flour
1 egg, unbeaten	½ teaspoon salt
1 8½-ounce can crushed	¼ teaspoon nutmeg
pineapple, undrained	1 teaspoon baking soda
½ cup chopped pecans	

Make day before:
1. Start heating oven to 375°F.
2. With mixer at medium speed, beat butter with sugar and egg until very light. Add pineapple and nuts.
3. Sift flour with salt, nutmeg, and baking soda. Blend into pineapple mixture.
4. Drop, by heaping tablespoonfuls, 2½ inches apart, onto lightly-greased cookie sheets.
5. Bake 10 to 15 minutes, or until golden.
6. Remove to wire rack; cool. Makes about 3 dozen.

PINEAPPLE-SPICE DROP COOKIES

2 cups sifted regular all-	½ cup brown sugar, packed
purpose flour	1 teaspoon cinnamon
1 teaspoon double-acting	½ teaspoon nutmeg
baking powder	¼ teaspoon ground cloves
1 teaspoon baking soda	1 egg, unbeaten
1 teaspoon salt	⅔ cup drained, canned
½ cup soft shortening	crushed pineapple
½ cup granulated sugar	

1. Start heating oven to 375°F.
2. Sift flour with baking powder, baking soda, and salt.
3. In large bowl, mix shortening with granulated sugar, brown sugar, cinnamon, nutmeg, cloves, and egg until creamy. Blend in pineapple, then blend in flour mixture.
4. Drop, by rounded tablespoonfuls, 2 inches apart, onto ungreased cookie sheets.

5. Bake 12 to 15 minutes, or until lightly browned. Makes about 3½ dozen.

RAISIN-NUT COOKIES

1 cup undiluted evaporated	1 teaspoon allspice
milk	¼ teaspoon nutmeg
1 tablespoon vinegar	½ cup soft shortening
2 cups sifted regular all-	2 cups brown sugar, packed
purpose flour	2 eggs, unbeaten
1 teaspoon baking soda	3 cups dark or light raisins
½ teaspoon salt	1 cup chopped walnuts
1 teaspoon cinnamon	Browned-Butter Icing, below
1 teaspoon ground cloves	

1. Start heating oven to 350°F.
2. Into evaporated milk, stir vinegar; set aside.
3. Sift flour with baking soda, salt, cinnamon, cloves, allspice, and nutmeg.
4. Mix shortening, brown sugar, and eggs until light and fluffy. Blend in evaporated-milk mixture, then flour mixture. Stir in raisins and nuts.
5. Drop, by level tablespoonfuls, 2 inches apart, onto greased cookie sheets.
6. Bake about 15 minutes, or until done.
7. Cool; then frost with Browned-Butter Icing. Makes about 6 dozen.

BROWNED-BUTTER ICING: In heavy skillet, lightly brown ¾ cup butter or margarine (watch carefully to prevent burning). Blend in 3 cups sifted confectioners' sugar, 3 tablespoons undiluted evaporated milk, and 1½ teaspoons vanilla extract.

FRENCH TUILES

¾ cup (5 or 6) egg whites,	¼ cup lukewarm melted
unbeaten	shortening
1⅔ cups granulated sugar	1 cup sifted regular all-
¼ teaspoon salt	purpose flour
¾ cup lukewarm melted	¾ cup finely-chopped
butter or margarine	blanched almonds

1. Start heating oven to 350°F.
2. In large bowl, beat egg whites with sugar and salt until sugar is dissolved, and mixture is thick. Add butter and shortening; beat well. Add flour and almonds; mix well.
3. Drop, by level tablespoonfuls, 5 inches apart, onto ungreased cookie sheets.
4. Bake 8 to 10 minutes, or until done.
5. Let stand ½ minute; then quickly and gently remove, one at a time, and mold into half circle over rolling pin. Repeat with rest of mixture. Makes about 5 dozen.
Note: Bake only a few cookies at a time. If they harden before you can mold them, soften them in the oven. These keep a week or so.

SPICE-COOKIE LOLLIPOPS
(Pictured on page 12)

½ cup butter or margarine
½ cup granulated sugar
1 egg, unbeaten
½ cup molasses
2½ cups sifted regular all-
  purpose flour
¼ teaspoon salt
1 teaspoon baking soda
1 teaspoon ginger
½ teaspoon cinnamon
½ teaspoon ground cloves

½ teaspoon nutmeg
¼ cup lukewarm water
About 2 dozen wooden
  skewers, 4½ inches long
  (lollipop sticks)*
Confectioners' sugar
Red and green food color
About 48 semisweet-
  chocolate pieces
About 24 tiny red gumdrops

Make several days ahead:
1.   In medium bowl, with mixer at medium speed, beat
butter with granulated sugar until light and fluffy. Add
egg; beat well, then beat in molasses.
2.   Sift flour with salt, baking soda, ginger, cinnamon,
cloves, and nutmeg. Add to sugar mixture, alternately
with water, at low speed, and beating smooth after each
addition.
3.   Start heating oven to 375°F.
4.   Drop batter, by heaping tablespoonfuls, about 4
inches apart, onto ungreased cookie sheet. Insert a lollipop stick into each with a twisting motion.
5.   Bake about 10 minutes.
6.   Let cool on cookie sheet 1 minute, then remove to
wire racks to finish cooling.
7.   When cool, frost, as pictured, with confectioners'
sugar mixed with a little water, then tinted pink or
green. Decorate with chocolate pieces as eyes, tips of red
gumdrops for noses, and rest of red gumdrops for
mouths. Makes about 2 dozen.
*Available at meat markets.

TRIPLE TREATS

2½ cups sifted regular all-
  purpose flour
2 teaspoons double-acting
  baking powder
1 teaspoon salt
1 cup soft shortening
½ cup granulated sugar
½ cup light-brown sugar,
  packed
2 eggs, unbeaten
1 teaspoon vanilla extract

½ cup milk
1 teaspoon cinnamon
½ cup finely-snipped
  pitted dates
1 teaspoon almond extract
1 envelope (1 ounce)
  no-melt unsweetened
  chocolate
1 tablespoon water
½ cup flaked coconut
Few maraschino cherries

Make, freeze dough up to 1 month ahead:
1.   Sift flour with baking powder and salt.
2.   In large bowl, with mixer at high speed, cream
shortening until light and fluffy. At medium speed, add
granulated sugar and brown sugar, beating until well
blended. Beat in eggs and vanilla until well blended.

3.   At low speed, ad...
then rest of flour.
4.   Place dough in freezer c...
freeze.
On baking day:
1.   Allow unwrapped dough to thaw a...
ature until pliable. Divide into three equal p...
2.   Start heating oven to 400°F.
3.   Into first third of dough stir cinnamon and da...
To second third of dough add almond extract. To last
third, add no-melt chocolate, water, and coconut.
4.   For each cookie, drop about a half teaspoonful of
each dough onto greased cookie sheets so that three
doughs just touch each other, forming a triangle. Top
almond-flavored portion of dough with sliver of maraschino cherry.
5.   Bake 10 to 12 minutes, or until lightly browned
and done.
6.   Remove to wire racks to cool. Store in tightly-covered container. Makes about 4 dozen.

YUM-YUMS
(Pictured on page 12)

1 cup vegetable shortening
1½ cups granulated sugar
3 eggs, unbeaten
3 cups sifted regular all-
  purpose flour
1 teaspoon baking soda
1 teaspoon cinnamon

¼ teaspoon salt
1 tablespoon water
1 8-ounce package pitted
  dates, snipped
1 cup coarsely-broken
  walnuts

Early on day:
1.   In large bowl, with mixer at medium speed, blend
shortening with sugar until light and fluffy; beat in
eggs one at a time.
2.   Start heating oven to 375°F.
3.   Onto waxed paper, sift flour with baking soda,
cinnamon, and salt; then beat into sugar mixture.
3.   Add water to dates; stir dates and nuts into flour
mixture.
4.   Drop, by heaping teaspoonfuls, onto greased cookie
sheets.
5.   Bake 12 to 15 minutes.
6.   Remove to wire racks to cool. Makes about 6 dozen.

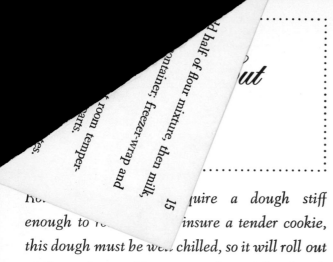

...ll half of flour mixture, then milk, ... container; freezer-wrap and ...room temper...arts. ...es. 15

...quire a dough stiff enough to re... ... insure a tender cookie, this dough must be well chilled, so it will roll out easily without adding more flour. The dough should be handled a little at a time with the remaining dough left to continue chilling in the refrigerator. When rolling, use a rolling pin covered with a lightly-floured stockinet. Cut the cookies close together to get more from the first rolling; rerolled cookies will not be as tender as those from the first rolling.

SUGAR SHAPES
(Pictured on page 12)

⅔ cup salad oil	3 cups sifted regular all-
1½ cups granulated sugar	purpose flour
2 eggs, unbeaten	2 teaspoons double-acting
1 tablespoon grated lemon	baking powder
peel	1 teaspoon salt
1 tablespoon lemon juice	1 teaspoon mace
	Ornamental Frosting, below

Make several days ahead or early on day:
1. In large bowl combine salad oil and sugar. With mixer at medium speed, beat until well blended. Add eggs, one at a time, beating well after each addition. Then, with mixer at low speed blend in lemon peel and juice.
2. Sift flour with baking powder, salt, and mace. Beat into batter until well blended. Refrigerate at least one hour, wrapped in foil or saran.
3. Start heating oven to 375°F.
4. On lightly floured surface, roll out dough, one-third at a time, to about ⅛-inch thickness. Cut into desired shapes with floured cookie cutters. Place on ungreased cookie sheets.

5. Bake 7 to 10 minutes, or until light browned.
6. Remove from cookie sheeets; cool on wire racks.
7. Meanwhile, make Ornamental Frosting. Divide frosting into three bowls; tint one green, one red, and leave one white. Decorate cookies as desired, either by spreading frosting on cookies with small spatula, or by putting some frosting through decorating tube with small, round (number 2) decorating tip. Frosting on cookies becomes very hard when dry. Store in loosely-covered container. Makes about 5 to 6 dozen.

STARRY DELIGHTS: Make Sugar Shapes dough as above, but cut with small star-shaped cutter in step 4. Tint Ornamental Frosting red before using to frost stars.

ORNAMENTAL FROSTING: Into medium bowl sift 1 1-pound package confectioners' sugar with ½ teaspoon cream of tartar. With mixer at medium speed, mix in 3 egg whites, then ½ teaspoon vanilla extract. Beat until so stiff that knife drawn through mixture leaves clean-cut path. Cover with a damp cloth.

SUGAR COOKIES

4 cups sifted cake flour	1½ cups granulated sugar
2½ teaspoons double-	2 eggs, unbeaten
acting baking powder	1 teaspoon vanilla extract
½ teaspoon salt	4 teaspoons milk
⅔ cup soft shortening	

1. Sift flour with baking powder and salt.
2. Mix shortening with sugar, eggs, and vanilla until *very light and fluffy.* Mix in flour alternately with milk.
3. Refrigerate dough until easy to handle (you may hasten this by placing dough in freezing compartment).
4. Start heating oven to 400°F.
5. On lightly floured surface, roll out dough, one-half or one-third at a time, to ⅛- or ¼-inch thickness. For crisp cookies, roll dough paper thin. Keep remaining dough in refrigerator.
6. With floured cookie cutter or cardboard pattern, cut into desired shapes, keeping cuttings close together.
7. With broad spatula, place cookies, ½-inch apart, on lightly greased cookie sheets. If desired, brush with cream or with egg white diluted with water. Then, if desired, sprinkle with white or colored sugar, chopped nuts, flaked coconut, cut-up gumdrops, silver dragées, combined cinnamon and sugar, bits of candied fruits, etc.
8. Bake 9 minutes, or until delicate brown. Makes about 6 dozen.

BUTTERSCOTCH-PECAN COOKIES: Substitute 2 cups brown sugar, packed, for granulated sugar. Add 1 cup finely-chopped pecans with flour mixture in step 2.

LEMON SUGAR COOKIES: Substitute 4 teaspoons lemon juice and 2 tablespoons grated lemon peel for vanilla.

SUGAR-COOKIE DANGLES (Pictured here): Make Sugar-Cookie dough as directed on page 16. Also, make a second batch, adding 4 squares melted unsweetened chocolate with shortening in step 2. Refrigerate both doughs. Meanwhile, draw, then cut out a cardboard pattern in the shape of a Christmas-tree ornament about 2½ inches wide by 4½ inches high. Roll out vanilla dough to ⅛-inch thickness; cut around cardboard pattern; place on lightly-greased cookie sheets. Then, with flat end of a wooden skewer, make a ⅛-inch hole about 1 inch down from top of each cookie. Bake 6 minutes, or until lightly browned. Remove to wire rack to cool. Repeat with chocolate-cookie dough. Cool; then store in tightly-covered container until ready to decorate. Makes about 148 cookies.

To decorate:

Make ½ recipe for Ornamental Frosting, page 16. With red food color, tint one-third bright red, leaving rest of frosting white. With some of each frosting in a wax-paper cone or decorating bag, and decorating tubes numbers 2 and 3 or 4, decorate cookies as pictured, adding silver dragées and tiny red cinnamon candies, if desired. For each Sugar-Cookie Dangle, string 6 to 12 cookies, each on a different length of gold cord or red ribbon; also string a pair of child's scissors. Fasten lengths together at top with holly tied with red ribbon. Place each dangle in a long box with 2 dozen or more cookie ornaments, then wrap. Extra cookies are for replenishing dangles as they are needed. Makes 4 Sugar-Cookie Dangles.

ALMOND-STUDDED ANGEL WINGS (Pictured on page 54): Make ½ recipe for Sugar-Cookie dough, page 16, adding 2 envelopes (2 ounces) no-melt unsweetened chocolate with shortening in step 2. On greased, lightly floured cookie sheets, roll out dough to paper-thinness, using one-half or one-third at a time. With 9-inch layer-cake pan as a guide, cut out circle with fluted pastry wheel. Then, with pastry wheel, divide circle into 6 wedges, removing trimmings to reroll. Repeat with remaining dough. Bake about 9 minutes. Cool on wire racks. Meanwhile, make Rum Butter Cream, below. Also, toast 2 4½-ounce cans whole blanched almonds, halved, on cookie sheet in 400°F. oven 5 minutes; do not overbrown. Spread some of butter cream on flat side of each almond half; then lay on wings as pictured; dip edges of wings in confectioners' sugar. Refrigerate in loosely-covered container. Makes 2 dozen.

RUM BUTTER CREAM: With mixer at medium speed, combine ⅓ cup butter or margarine with ⅛ teaspoon salt and 1 cup sifted confectioners' sugar until light. Add 2 cups sifted confectioners' sugar alternately with ⅛ to ¼ cup rum, beating until of spreading consistency. Reserve excess for Pecan-Centered Christmas Stars, page 57, if desired.

Sugar-Cookie Dangles

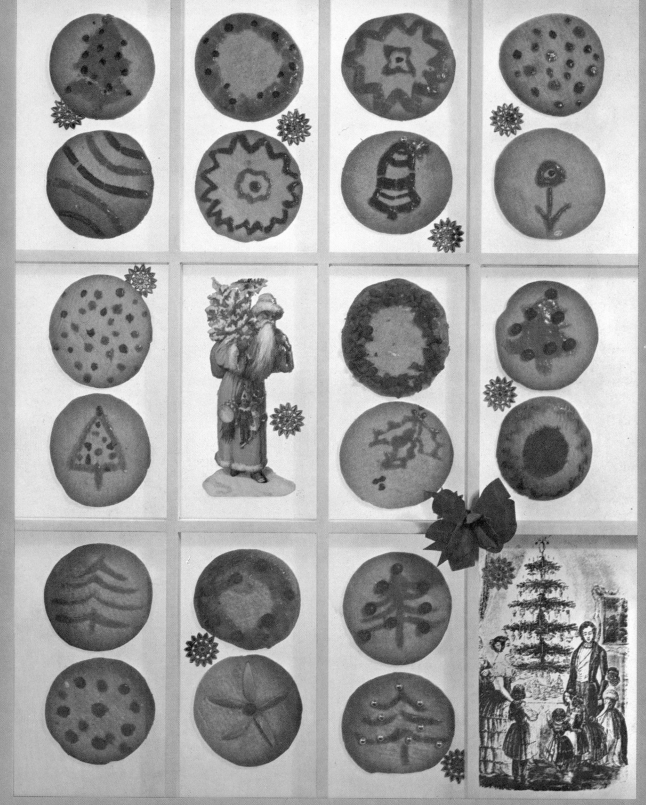

Cookie Sketches

COOKIE SKETCHES
(Pictured opposite)

¾ cup sifted confectioners' sugar	1¼ cups sifted regular all-purpose flour
½ cup butter or maragarine	½ teaspoon baking soda
1 egg, unbeaten	½ teaspoon cream of tartar
½ teaspoon vanilla extract	Egg-Yolk Paint, below
¼ teaspoon almond extract	

Make up to 2 weeks ahead, if desired:
1. In small bowl, with mixer at medium speed, beat sugar with butter until creamy; add egg, vanilla, and almond extract; beat well.
2. Sift flour with baking soda and cream of tartar. With mixer at low speed, beat into sugar mixture. Divide dough in half; refrigerate 2 to 3 hours, or until stiff.
3. Start heating oven to 375°F.
4. On well-floured surface, roll out half of dough to ⅛-inch thickness. Cut with 2¼-inch floured round cookie cutter; place on lightly greased cookie sheets. Repeat.
5. Paint with Egg-Yolk Paint as pictured, or in your own way.
6. Bake 7 to 8 minutes.
7. Cool on wire racks; store in loosely-covered container. Makes about 2 dozen.

EGG-YOLK PAINT: With fork or wire whip, mix 1 egg yolk with ¼ teaspoon water. Divide among several custard cups or paper cups. Add a few drops of a different liquid food color to each cup, to tint as desired. With small paintbrushes, a separate one for each color, paint unbaked cookies.

Note: Our Cookie Sketches were designed for the Holiday Season, but these cookies are equally good for other occasions. In shaping and decorating, let your imagination be your guide.

NORWEGIAN SUGAR COOKIES

2 cups sifted regular all-purpose flour	1 cup granulated sugar
2 teaspoons double-acting baking powder	1 egg, well beaten
¼ teaspoon salt	3 tablespoons brandy
½ cup shortening	1½ teaspoons caraway seeds
	Confectioners' sugar

1. Sift flour with baking powder and salt.
2. Work shortening with a spoon until fluffy and creamy. Gradually add sugar, while continuing to work until light. Beat in egg. Stir flour mixture and brandy into shortening mixture. Then stir in caraway seeds. Refrigerate until firm enough to handle easily—about 1 hour.
3. Start heating oven to 350°F.
4. On lightly floured surface, roll out dough to ⅛-

inch thickness or thinner. Cut into small stars, circles, etc. Place, ½ inch apart, on greased cookie sheets. Sprinkle with confectioners' sugar.
5. Bake 6 to 8 minutes, or until light brown. Makes about 12 dozen.

CREAM WAFERS

1¼ cups soft butter or margarine	Granulated sugar
⅓ cup heavy cream	¾ cup confectioners' sugar
2 cup sifted regular all-purpose flour	1 egg yolk, beaten
	1 teaspoon vanilla extract

1. In large bowl, with mixer at low speed, beat 1 cup butter with cream and flour until creamy; refrigerate 4 hours, or until firm enough to roll out.
2. Start heating oven to 375°F.
3. On floured, cloth-covered surface, roll out one third of dough at a time (keep rest refrigerated) to ⅛ inch thickness. With floured 1½-inch cookie cutter, cut into rounds; transfer rounds to wax paper, covered with granulated sugar. Place on ungreased cookie sheets. With fork, prick each round about 4 times.
4. Bake 7 to 9 minutes; then remove at once to wire racks; cool.
5. Meanwhile, in small bowl, beat confectioners' sugar gradually into ¼ cup butter until fluffy; beat in egg yolk and vanilla until smooth; refrigerate this filling.
6. To serve, put wafers together in pairs with filling between. Makes about 40.

BOW-TIED HOLIDAY WREATHS
(Pictured on page 54)

1 cup butter or margarine	2½ cups instant-type flour*
¾ cup granulated sugar	1 egg, beaten
5 sieved hard-cooked egg yolks	Colored sugars
1 tablespoon grated orange peel	Dragées
	Cinnamon candies

Make up to 2 weeks ahead, if desired:
1. In large bowl, with mixer at medium speed, beat butter with sugar until light and fluffy; beat in sieved egg yolks and orange peel. Gradually beat in flour, blending well. Wrap dough in foil or saran; refrigerate overnight.
About 15 minutes before baking:
1. Remove dough from refrigerator.
2. Start heating oven to 350°F.
3. On lightly-floured, cloth-covered surface, roll out half of dough to ⅜-inch thickness. With floured 4-inch round cookie cutter, cut out cookies. With broad spatula, transfer to ungreased cookie sheets, 2 inches apart. Repeat.
4. About ¾ inch in from edge, using floured 1-inch

round cookie cutter, cut a circle in each cookie, removing dough carefully (use later with other trimmings). Brush cookies with beaten egg diluted with a little water; sprinkle around edges with colored sugars, dragées, and cinnamon candies.

5. Bake 8 to 10 minutes, or until golden.

6. Cool on wire racks. If desired, hang on Christmas tree by narrow ribbons as pictured. Makes about 20. *Do not sift this flour.

IRIDESCENT ALMOND STRAWS (Pictured on page 54): Make dough as directed above, substituting 2½ cups sifted regular all-purpose flour for instant-type. Roll dough to ⅛-inch thickness. With pastry wheel, cut into strips 8-inches by ¾-inch. Arrange on ungreased cookie sheet. Brush with beaten egg, diluted with a little water; then sprinkle with multicolored candy sprinkles and coarsely-chopped almonds. Bake 8 minutes, or to delicate brown. Cool on wire racks. Repeat. Makes about 3 dozen.

COOKIE SANDWICHES

2½ cups sifted regular all-purpose flour	½ cup sifted confectioners' sugar
¼ teaspoon double-acting baking powder	2 tablespoons milk
½ teaspoon salt	Half and half
1 cup soft shortening	Blanched almonds
2 teaspoons vanilla extract	Currant jelly

1. Sift flour with baking powder and salt.

2. In large bowl, mix together shortening, vanilla, and sugar until *very light and fluffy*. Mix in flour mixture and milk. Refrigerate until easy to handle.

3. Start heating oven to 350°F.

4. On lightly-floured surface, roll out dough to ¼-inch thickness. Cut into 2½-inch rounds. Cut ¾-inch circle from center of each of half of rounds. Brush with half and half; shave on a few almonds. Place on ungreased cookie sheet, 1 inch apart.

5. Bake 15 minutes, or until done.

6. Cool on wire racks. Place 1 teaspoon jelly in centers of flat sides of whole rounds; top with rings, with right sides up. Makes 1 dozen.

SPRINGERLE

4½ cups sifted cake flour	1 1-pound package confectioners' sugar, sifted
1 teaspoon double-acting baking powder	1 tablespoon grated lemon peel
4 eggs, unbeaten	Anise seeds

Make 2 or 3 weeks ahead:

1. Sift flour with baking powder.

2. In large bowl, with mixer at medium speed, beat

eggs until light. Gradually add sugar, beating well. With wooden spoon, blend in lemon peel and flour mixture. Wrap dough in foil or saran; refrigerate 1 hour.

3. On lightly-floured surface, with floured springerle form, or rolling pin, roll out dough to ½-inch thickness, printing pictures on surface. With sharp knife, cut out cookies on lines between pictures.

4. Arrange on greased cookie sheets that have been sprinkled generously with anise seeds. Let stand on cookie sheets at room temperature at least 12 hours.

5. Bake at 325°F. 25 to 30 minutes.

6. Cool, then store in tightly-covered container for two to three weeks before serving. Makes 40 cookies.

LAYERED RICKRACK RECTANGLES
(Pictured on page 54)

2 cups sifted regular all-purpose flour	1 teaspoon vanilla extract
½ teaspoon double-acting baking powder	Chocolate Glaze, page 21
¼ teaspoon salt	½ cup heavy cream
½ cup butter or margarine	Finely-chopped walnuts
1 cup granulated sugar	Slivered and halved blanched almonds
1 egg, unbeaten	Glacéed cherries

Make early on day:

1. Sift flour with baking powder and salt.

2. In medium bowl, with mixer at medium speed, beat butter with sugar until light and creamy. Beat in egg and vanilla, then flour mixture until smooth and blended. Refrigerate 1 hour.

3. Start heating oven to 400°F.

4. On lightly floured surface, roll out one-third of dough into rectangle 10½-by-9-inches. With fluted pastry wheel, cut it into 21 3-by-1½-inch rectangles. Arrange on greased cookie sheets.

5. Bake 6 minutes, or until golden around edges. Repeat twice more.

6. Meanwhile, make Chocolate Glaze. Spread thinly on one-third of cookies. Refrigerate rest of Glaze until cool; then, into it, fold cream, whipped. Spread on rest of cookies.

7. Stack cookies in threes, with a glazed cookie on top. Top with nuts and cherries, as pictured; refrigerate until served. Makes about 21.

CHOCOLATE GLAZE: In small bowl combine 2 tablespoons shortening, 2 envelopes (2 ounces) no-melt unsweetened chocolate, and 1 cup sifted confectioners' sugar; add boiling water, a tablespoon at a time, until mixture is of spreading consistency (about 2 to 4 tablespoons in all).

SWEETIES

2 cups sifted cake flour	1 cup ground blanched
¼ teaspoon salt	almonds
¼ teaspoon nutmeg	1½ teaspoons grated lemon
¾ cup granulated sugar	peel
¼ cup liquid honey	⅓ cup finely-cut mixed
1 egg, unbeaten	candied lemon and
	orange peels

Make 2 to 4 weeks ahead:

1. Sift flour with salt and nutmeg.
2. In medium bowl, combine sugar, honey, and egg. Stir in almonds, grated lemon peel, and lemon and orange peels. Gradually add flour mixture, stirring until well blended. Wrap dough in wax paper or saran; refrigerate at least 1 hour, or until easy to handle.
3. Start heating oven to 350°F.
4. On lightly-floured surface, roll out dough to ⅛-inch thickness. Cut into 2-inch rounds and/or 3-by-1½-inch rectangles. Place on greased cookie sheets.
5. Bake 10 to 12 minutes, or until done.
6. Cool on wire racks. Store in tightly-covered container for two to four weeks before serving. They keep well. Makes about 5 dozen.

CHRISTMAS BELLS
(Pictured on page 54)

½ cup butter or margarine	1½ teaspoons grated lemon
1¾ cups confectioners'	peel
sugar	Decorating Frosting,
2 eggs, unbeaten	page 27, or other
2 cups instant-type flour*	favorite frosting
¼ teaspoon cinnamon	Liquid food colors
½ teaspoon double-acting	Red and green tinted sugars
baking powder	Multicolored nonpareils
	Silver dragées

Make any time up to 2 weeks ahead:

1. In medium bowl, with mixer at medium speed, beat butter with sugar until creamy; beat in eggs, one at a time, beating well after each addition.
2. Stir flour with cinnamon and baking powder. Beat into sugar mixture with lemon peel. Refrigerate dough several hours, or overnight if possible; or put in freezer to firm up dough.

3. Meanwhile, from cardboard, cut a bell pattern, 4½ inches high by 3½ inches wide at widest point.
4. Start heating oven to 350°F.
5. On floured, cloth-covered surface, roll out one-half of dough as thinly as possible. Use floured bell pattern to cut out cookies, rerolling as needed. Place on well-greased cookie sheets. Repeat.
6. Bake 7 to 9 minutes.
7. Cool on wire racks. When cool, frost cookies as follows: Divide Decorating Frosting or other favorite frosting among 5 paper cups; to each add a few drops of a different food color. Using small paintbrushes, or pastry bag with plain writing tube number 5, decorate cookies; sprinkle with tinted sugars, nonpareils, or dragées, as pictured, or design your own. When set, store in loosely-covered container. Makes 4 dozen.
*Do not sift this flour.

GOLDEN ALMOND CRISPS
(Pictured on page 12)

1 cup butter, margarine,	½ teaspoon double-acting
or shortening	baking powder
1¼ cups granulated sugar	¼ teaspoon cinnamon
1 egg, slightly beaten	1 egg white, slightly beaten
1 tablespoon grated lemon	½ cup blanched almonds,
peel	finely chopped
2 tablespoons rum	Whole blanched almonds
3 cups sifted regular all-	(optional)
purpose flour	

Make several days ahead:

1. In large bowl, with mixer at medium speed, beat butter until light and fluffy; then gradually add 1 cup sugar, beating well. Add egg, lemon peel, and rum, blending well.
2. Sift flour with baking powder. With mixer at low speed, add, in fourths, to butter mixture. Refrigerate dough, covered with foil or saran, about 1 hour, or until easy to handle.
3. Meanwhile, combine ¼ cup sugar with cinnamon.
4. Start heating oven to 325°F.
5. On floured, cloth-covered surface, with floured stockinet-covered rolling pin, roll out small portion of chilled dough very thin (keep rest of dough refrigerated). Cut into 2-inch rounds, as pictured, or other shapes.
6. Place on ungreased cookie sheets. Brush with egg white; sprinkle with cinnamon-sugar, then with chopped almonds. Top each with whole almond, if desired.
7. Bake 10 to 12 minutes, or until lightly browned at edges.
8. Remove carefully to wire racks to cool. Repeat with rest of dough. Store in loosely-covered container. Makes about 5 dozen.

Lemon-Chiffon Chocolate Tarts, Swedish Double-Chocolate Rounds, Chocolate Fruit Cookie

SWEDISH DOUBLE-CHOCOLATE ROUNDS
(Pictured opposite)

¾ cup butter or margarine	¼ teaspoon almond extract
¾ cup granulated sugar	2½ cups sifted regular all-
1 egg, unbeaten	purpose flour
⅓ cup blanched almonds, ground	

Make cookies day before, if desired:
1. In large bowl, with mixer at low speed, cream butter with sugar until light and fluffy. Beat in egg, almonds, almond extract, then flour.
2. Start heating oven to 375°F.
3. On floured surface, roll out dough into a round, ¼ inch thick. With 2¾-inch round cookie cutter, cut out 30 cookies. Place on ungreased cookie sheets.
4. Bake about 12 minutes, or until lightly browned.
5. Cool on wire rack. Store, uncovered.

Make frosting and filling early on day:
1. In small, heavy saucepan, over low heat, place 1 ¼-pound bar German's sweet cooking chocolate and 2 tablespoons cold water. Stir constantly until chocolate melts; use to brush each cookie top generously. In the center of 15 of the cookies sprinkle a few slivered toasted almonds.
2. Sprinkle 1 envelope unflavored gelatin on ¼ cup cold water to soften; then stir over hot water until it is completely dissolved; cool.
3. In medium bowl, combine 1 cup heavy cream, ½ teaspoon vanilla extract, 1½ tablespoons cocoa, and cooled gelatin. With mixer at high speed, beat just until it holds soft peaks.
4. In another bowl, beat 2 egg whites until frothy; then beat in 6 tablespoons granulated sugar, one tablespoon at a time, until stiff peaks form. Fold into cocoa mixture; refrigerate until needed.

Just before serving:
On each plain cookie spread about 3 tablespoons cocoa mixture; cover with almond-topped cookie; repeat with all cookies. Serve at once. Makes 15.

LEMON-CHIFFON CHOCOLATE TARTS
(Pictured opposite)

1 recipe dough for Swedish Double-Chocolate Rounds, above	3 tablespoons water
	1 3-ounce package lemon-chiffon-pie-filling mix
2 ¼-pound bars German's sweet cooking chocolate	

Make tart shells day before, if desired:
1. Make up cookie dough as directed.
2. Start heating oven to 375°F.
3. On floured surface, roll out half of dough into ¼-inch-thick round. With floured 4-inch round cookie cutter, cut dough into 5 rounds. Now carefully fit each round over the outside of an ungreased 3¼-inch fluted tart pan so dough is about ¼ inch from edge of pan. Repeat with other half of dough.
4. Reroll "dough trimmings", then cut and shape 2 more 4-inch rounds over outside of tart pans as in step 3 above. Place all tart pans on cookie sheet.
5. Bake 15 to 20 minutes, or until light brown.
6. Cool; carefully remove from tart pans by pressing gently on edges of pans at top. Store, uncovered.

Early on day:
In small, heavy saucepan, over low heat, place 1½ bars of chocolate and water, stirring constantly until chocolate melts. Use to brush inside of each tart shell generously; set aside.

About 1¼ hours before serving:
Make pie-filling mix as label directs. Lightly pile in each tart shell up to ½ inch from top. Sprinkle with remaining ½ bar of chocolate, grated. Refrigerate until served. Makes 12.

CHOCOLATE FRUIT COOKIES
(Pictured opposite)

¾ cup butter or margarine	2½ cups sifted regular all-purpose flour
¾ cup granulated sugar	
1 egg, unbeaten	½ teaspoon vanilla extract
⅓ cup packaged fine-grated coconut	

Make cookies day before, if desired:
1. In large bowl, with mixer at low speed, cream butter with sugar until light and fluffy; beat in egg and coconut; blend will. Gradually beat in flour and vanilla.
2. Start heating oven to 375°F.
3. On floured surface, roll out dough into rectangle 18-by-12-inches-by-⅛-inch thick. Cut into 36 cookies, 3 inches by 2 inches. Place carefully on ungreased cookie sheets.
4. Bake about 12 minutes, or until lightly browned.
5. Cool on wire racks. Store, uncovered.

To top and decorate:
1. Drain 2 16-ounce cans cling-peach slices, reserving 1 cup juice. In small, heavy saucepan place 2 tablespoons cornstarch; stir in a little reserved juice; then stir in remaining juice and cook, stirring constantly, until thick and clear. Cool.
2. In second small, heavy saucepan, over low heat, place 1 ¼-pound bar German's sweet cooking chocolate and 2 tablespoons water; stir constantly until chocolate melts. Use to brush complete top of each cookie.
3. Now on each chocolate-glazed cookie, arrange a well-drained peach slice. Then top with either a drained, pitted prune half, or half a fresh strawberry. Next carefully spoon glaze over fruits and chocolate. Sprinkle edges of cookies with very finely chopped walnuts (you will need about 1 cup). Makes 36.

CINNAMON STARS

3 large egg whites
2½ cups sifted
  confectioners' sugar
½ teaspoon grated lemon
  peel

1 teaspoon cinnamon
2 cups ground blanched
  almonds
Confectioners' sugar

Make several days ahead:
1. In medium bowl, with mixer at high speed, beat egg whites until stiff but not dry; gradually beat in 2 cups sugar. Set aside ¾ cup of this meringue mixture for frosting stars.
2. To rest, add lemon peel, cinnamon, and almonds; blend well, adding ½ cup more sugar to make "dough" workable.
3. Start heating oven to 350°F.
4. On wax paper, well covered with confectioners' sugar, pat out one-third of "dough"; generously coat top with confectioners' sugar. Cover with wax paper, and roll out to ⅛-inch thickness. Peel off top paper and, with well-floured 2¾-inch star cutter, cut out stars. With broad spatula, place stars on well-greased cookie sheets.
5. Bake 10 to 12 minutes.
6. Cool, then frost each with some of meringue.
7. Return to 325°F. oven for 5 minutes, or until meringue is set but still white.
8. When cool, store in covered container; they keep well. Makes about 3 dozen.

ALMOND-STAR COOKIE TREE
(Pictured opposite)

1½ cups butter or
  margarine
1¾ cups granulated sugar
4 eggs
1½ teaspoons cinnamon
¼ teaspoon ground cloves
3 cups finely-ground
  unblanched almonds

5½ cups sifted regular all-
  purpose flour
1 tablespoon milk
½ cup blanched whole
  almonds
1 teaspoon confectioners'
  sugar

Make several days ahead:
1. In large bowl, with mixer at medium speed, beat butter well; then add granulated sugar gradually, beating until light. Add 3 unbeaten eggs and blend well. Add cinnamon, cloves, and ground almonds; blend well. Stir in flour and mix thoroughly. Wrap dough in wax paper or foil and refrigerate overnight.
2. Meanwhile, from cardboard, cut out eleven 8-pointed star patterns as follows: 10-inch star (measuring from point-to-point across center), 9½ inch star, 9-inch star, then 8½ inch, 8-inch, 7-inch, 6-inch, 5-inch, 4-inch, 3-inch, and 2-inch stars. Set aside.
Early next day:
2. On well-floured surface, with floured rolling pin,

roll out small portion of dough at a time to ¼-inch thickness (refrigerate remainder). Using cardboard stars, cut out 12 stars (make two of 2-inch size); then, with 1¾-inch round cookie cutter, cut out about 18 rounds.
3. With narrower end of number 9 pastry tube, cut a hole in center of all rounds and all but 2-inch stars.
4. With two broad floured spatulas, transfer cookies to ungreased cookie sheets.
5. Mix milk with one beaten egg, then use to brush stars and rounds thoroughly.
6. Split whole almonds lengthwise. Place one almond half on points of all but 2-inch stars, as pictured. To decorate 2-inch stars, cut each of four almonds into four lengthwise pieces.
7. Bake round cookies 20 minutes; bake stars 30 minutes.
8. Cool on wire racks. Store in tightly-covered container in cool place.
To make tree:
1. You will need a 9-inch wooden hat stand with dowel about ¾ inch thick. Prepare hat stand by taking top off dowel and, with ice pick or small nail, making a 1-inch deep hole in center top. Slip one or two round cookies onto dowel, then the 10-inch star; then another round cookie, then the 9½ inch star, then a round cookie, and repeat with round cookies and stars until only the 2-inch stars are left.
2. Mix confectioners' sugar with a few drops water. Use to glue the 2-inch stars together sandwich fashion. Let dry.
3. Insert one end of a wooden pick into hole in top of dowel, the other end between the joined stars; holding them upright as pictured. Trim off pick if necessary. Makes 1 cookie tree.

CRESCENT MELTAWAYS
(Pictured on page 8)

1 8-ounce package creamed
  cottage cheese
1 cup butter or margarine
  (½ pound)
2 cups sifted regular
  all-purpose flour
¼ cup melted butter or
  margarine

¾ cup light-brown sugar
Dash cinnamon
¾ cup finely-chopped
  walnuts
1 egg yolk, unbeaten
2 tablespoons water

Make day before, if desired, or early on day:
1. In medium bowl, with pastry fork, blend cottage cheese with 1 cup butter. Sift in flour, then blend until dough forms a ball.
2. Start heating oven to 400°F.
3. Divide dough in thirds. On lightly-floured, cloth-covered surface, roll out one-third of dough to ⅛-inch thickness, and circular in shape.

Almond-Star Cookie Tree

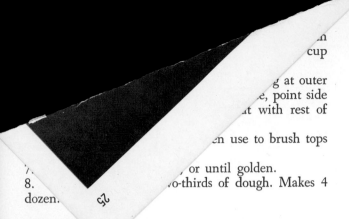

...n
... cup

... g at outer
... e, point side
... it with rest of

... en use to brush tops

7. ... , or until golden.
8. ... o-thirds of dough. Makes 4 dozen.

PRINTEN...

2¼ cups sifted regular all-purpose flour	*2 tablespoons butter or margarine*
3 teaspoons double-acting baking powder	*Milk*
¾ teaspoon cinnamon	*¼ teaspoon lemon extract*
¾ teaspoon ground cloves	*¾ teaspoon crushed anise seeds*
½ cup dark corn syrup	*1 cup confectioners' sugar*
3 tablespoons granulated sugar	*1 tablespoon water*

Make several weeks ahead:

1. Sift flour with baking powder, cinnamon, and cloves.
2. In saucepan, combine corn syrup, granulated sugar, butter, and 2 tablespoons milk. Cook, over low heat, until dissolved and melted, stirring occasionally; cool. Stir in lemon extract, anise seeds, and half of flour mixture. Add rest of flour mixture; refrigerate 1 hour.
3. Start heating oven to 400°F.
4. On floured surface, with floured rolling pin, roll out dough ¼ inch thick. Cut into rectangles 3½ by 2 inches; brush with milk. Place on greased cookie sheet.
5. Bake 10 minutes.
6. Cool, then frost with confectioners' sugar beaten smooth with water. When set, store in tightly-covered container; they keep indefinitely. (To hasten softening, add ½ apple.) Makes 18.

SCOTCH SHORTBREAD

2 cups sifted regular all-purpose flour	*¼ teaspoon salt*
¼ teaspoon double-acting baking powder	*1 cup soft butter or margarine*
	½ cup confectioners' sugar

1. Sift flour with baking powder and salt.
2. Mix butter with sugar until *very light and fluffy*. Mix in flour mixture. Refrigerate until firm enough to handle easily.
3. Start heating oven to 350°F.
4. On lightly-floured surface, roll out dough to ¼ inch thickness. Cut into diamonds, squares, triangles, etc. Place, 1 inch apart, on ungreased cookie sheet. Or pat chilled dough into 9-by-9-by-2-inch baking pan. Sprinkle with a cinnamon-and-sugar mixture, if desired.
5. Bake 20 to 25 minutes, or until done.
6. If baked in pan, cut into desired shapes while still warm. Remove to wire racks to cool. Makes about 2½ dozen.

WALNUT SHORTBREAD: Substitute ⅔ cup brown sugar, packed, for confectioners' sugar. Add ¾ cup finely chopped walnuts. Decorate cookies with walnut halves or candied cherries. Bake at 300°F. 20 to 25 minutes.

ELLEN'S GINGERSNAPS

½ cup maple syrup	*1 teaspoon grated lemon peel*
½ cup butter or margarine	*1 tablespoon dark rum*
⅓ cup brown sugar, firmly packed	*1 teaspoon baking soda*
1 teaspoon ginger	*2½ cups sifted regular all-purpose flour*
1 teaspoon cinnamon	
1 teaspoon ground cloves	

Make several weeks ahead, if desired, or day before:

1. In saucepan combine maple syrup, butter, and brown sugar; boil until butter and sugar are melted. Stir in ginger, cinnamon, cloves, lemon peel, rum, and baking soda. Remove from heat; pour into large bowl, cool until lukewarm.
2. When mixture is lukewarm, gradually stir in flour. Wrap dough in wax paper; refrigerate until dough is easy to handle.
3. Start heating oven to 350°F.
4. Remove small portion of dough from refrigerator. On lightly-floured surface, roll out paper thin. Cut into desired shapes; place on greased cookie sheets.
5. Bake 5 to 8 minutes, or until done.
6. Cool on wire racks.
7. Repeat with rest of dough as desired. These cookies may be stored several weeks in tightly-covered container. Makes about 8½ dozen 2½-inch cookies.

GINGERBREAD BOYS

(Pictured on page 12)

2 cups sifted regular all-purpose flour	*1½ teaspoons cinnamon*
½ teaspoon salt	*½ teaspoon nutmeg*
½ teaspoon baking soda	*½ cup vegetable shortening*
1 teaspoon double-acting baking powder	*½ cup granulated sugar*
1 teaspoon ginger	*½ cup molasses*
1 teaspoon ground cloves	*1 egg yolk, unbeaten*
	Decorating Frosting, page 27
	Red cinnamon candies

Make early on day:

1. Onto wax paper sift flour with salt, baking soda, baking powder, ginger, cloves, cinnamon, and nutmeg.

2. In bowl cream shortening with sugar and molasses until light and fluffy; beat in egg yolk, then flour mixture.

3. Start heating oven to 350°F.

4. On lightly-floured surface, roll out dough ¼ inch thick. Using floured gingerbread-boy cutter, cut out cookies. Place on ungreased cookie sheets.

5. Bake 8 to 10 minutes.

6. Cool on wire racks. Meanwhile, make Decorating Frosting.

7. When cool, decorate boys this way: With decorating bag and plain tube number 4, use frosting to make eyes, nose, mouth, and bowtie, as pictured. Also make 3 small white buttons on each, then press a cinnamon candy on each button. Makes 24 5-inch boys.

DECORATING FROSTING: Into small bowl sift 1¼ cups sifted confectioners' sugar with ⅛ teaspoon cream of tartar; add 1 egg white and ¼ teaspoon vanilla extract; with mixer at high speed, beat until frosting holds its shape. Cover with a damp cloth.

GINGER COOKIES

½ cup heavy cream, whipped	1½ teaspoons ginger
1¼ cups dark-brown sugar, packed	1½ teaspoons grated lemon peel
½ cup molasses	4½ cups sifted regular all-purpose flour
2 tablespoons water	Blanched almonds, halved
1 tablespoon baking soda	Icing, below

Make 2 or 3 weeks ahead, if desired:

1. In large bowl, with wooden spoon, stir together whipped cream, brown sugar, molasses, water, baking soda, ginger, and lemon peel until well blended.

2. Gradually stir in flour until well blended and smooth. Refrigerate 3 hours; or wrap dough in wax paper, saran, or foil, then refrigerate until needed.

Just before baking:

1. Remove dough from refrigerator; let stand at room temperature about 20 minutes.

2. Start heating oven to 300°F.

3. On lightly-floured, cloth-covered surface, with a well-floured, stockinet-covered rolling pin, roll out one-fourth of dough to ⅛-inch thickness. With floured cookie cutters, cut out cookies; place, ½ inch apart, on lightly-greased cookie sheets. Top some of cookies with almond halves. Brush all with cold water.

4. Bake 10 to 15 minutes, or until done.

5. Cool on cookie sheets; remove to wire rack. Repeat with rest of dough.

6. Meanwhile, make icing. With decorating bag and tube number 4 in place, use icing to decorate cookies that do not have almonds with zigzag or straight lines and small dots. Let icing dry. Store cookies in tightly-covered container. These keep well. Makes 9 dozen.

ICING: In bowl, gradually stir 4 cups sifted confectioners' sugar into 2 egg whites until smooth. Cover with wax paper until needed.

LOVEBIRD PLACE-CARDS: Make one-half recipe dough for Ginger Cookies, above; refrigerate. Cut a cardboard pattern of a lovebird, 3 inches high and 1½ inches wide, using the illustration below as a guide. Roll out dough ⅛ inch thick; with cardboard pattern cut out 36 lovebirds. Bake as directed. Store in tightly-covered container until ready to decorate.

To decorate:

1. With 8-by-4-inch pieces of different colored construction paper, make a cone for each cookie bird, trimming it to an even 2½ inches across base and 4 inches high; secure with cellophane tape. Snip off about 1 inch at top of each so stem of bird will fit down into it.

2. Make Ornamental Frosting, page 16. With decorating bag and tube number 2, use frosting to decorate birds. On each paper cone, write name of guest with frosting. Insert lovebirds in cones; arrange on table as place-cards. Makes 36 birds.

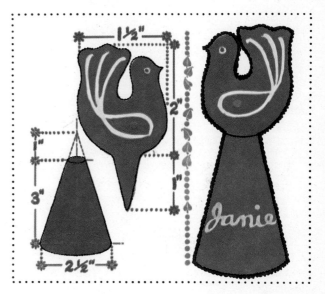

RUDOLPH CENTERPIECE (Pictured on page 28): A week or so ahead, make one-half recipe dough for Ginger Cookies, above; refrigerate. With tracing paper, trace our pictured reindeer, making legs about one inch longer; cut out a cardboard pattern. Roll out dough ⅛ inch thick; cut out 4 Rudolphs, 2 facing right and 2 facing left. Place on greased cookie sheet. Brush lower inch of legs with egg white, rest of bodies with cold water. Bake as directed. With 1½-inch round cookie cutter, cut out 4 cookie "wheels." Then with 2½-inch cutter, cut rounds from rest of dough. Bake as directed. Store Rudolphs, "wheels," and rounds in tightly-covered container until ready to decorate.

Rudolph Centerpiece

To decorate:
1. Make Ornamental Frosting, page 16. Press tiny bits of colored gumdrops on body of each Rudolph; with decorating bag and tube number 2, pipe frosting around each gumdrop as pictured.
2. When frosting is dry, fit two reindeer back to back for centerpiece, "gluing" them together with frosting. (Other two reindeer are for eating.)
3. Decorate cookie "wheels" as pictured, attaching rounded tops of small gumdrops in centers. Decorate 2½-inch rounds (for eating) as desired. Store rounds in tightly-covered container.
4. From a 1-pound 1½-ounce homemade or bakers'

poundcake, 6 by 3 by 3 inches, cut a lengthwise slice about ½ inch thick, forming the wagon on which Rudolph will stand.
5. Make one-half recipe for Ornamental Frosting, page 16; use to frost entire wagon. Decorate sides of wagon as pictured, attaching halves of small gumdrops.
6. Make two slits in top of wagon for Rudolph's legs; fill slits with frosting, then gently, but firmly insert Rudolph's legs into slits. Support legs front and back with wooden picks. Set aside to dry.
7. "Glue" cookie "wheels" to wagon with frosting as pictured. Use Rudolph as centerpiece; serve decorated rounds for nibbling.

GOLDEN COOKIE CONE (Pictured on page 30): From a piece of brown paper 32 inches long and 17 inches wide, cut a semicircle with a radius of 16 inches. Using this brown paper pattern, cut a semicircle from a piece of small-mesh 20-gauge chicken wire, 32 inches long and 17 inches wide. Shape this into a cone 12 inches across its base and 16 inches high, using pliers to join ends together; trim as needed to stand evenly. Now, with brown paper pattern, cut a semicircle from a piece of gold paper 31 inches long by 16 inches wide. Shape into a cone, securing seams with cellophane tape. Spray chicken-wire cone with metallic gold paint as label directs. When paint is dry insert gold-paper cone into chicken-wire cone, holding it in place by bending wire back over it at base.

For cookies:
1. Make dough for Ginger Cookies, page 27; refrigerate.
2. Roll out dough as directed; with favorite cookie cutters or cardboard patterns, cut out 50 to 60 cookies, making a hole in the top of each cookie with flat end of a wooden skewer.
3. Bake as directed. When cool, store *flat,* tightly covered, until ready to decorate.

To decorate:
1. Make twice recipe for Ornamental Frosting, page 16. Tint one-fourth light pink, one-fourth dark pink, one-fourth pale green; leave rest white.
2. One by one, frost and decorate cookies, using some of each of the four tinted frostings in decorating bag and tubes numbers 2, 3, and 4. Add silver dragées and colored sugars, if desired. Keep holes free of frosting.
3. With elastic gold cord, tie decorated cookies to wire cone as pictured. "Glue" a frosted cookie star to top of cone with frosting. Use as centerpiece; any extra cookies are for nibbling.

MOCHA JUMBLES

1½ cups sifted regular all-purpose flour	2 tablespoons soft shortening
1 tablespoon instant coffee powder	½ cup granulated sugar
2 teaspoons double-acting baking powder	1 egg, unbeaten
½ teaspoon cinnamon	1 tablespoon cold water
	1 square unsweetened chocolate, melted

Make a day or so ahead:
1. Sift flour with instant coffee powder, baking powder, and cinnamon.
2. In bowl, with mixer at medium speed (or with spoon), thoroughly mix shortening with sugar, then with egg and water, until *very light and fluffy.* Mix in chocolate. At low speed, beat in flour mixture.
3. Wrap dough in wax paper. Refrigerate until firm enough to roll out.

4. Start heating oven to 350°F.
5. On lightly floured surface, roll out dough very thin —about ⅛ inch thick. Cut with doughnut or cookie cutter. Sprinkle with a small amount of granulated sugar. Place on greased cookie sheet.
6. Bake 10 minutes. Makes 2½ dozen.

MOLASSES JINGLES

½ cup soft shortening	½ teaspoon baking soda
¼ cup soft butter or margarine	½ teaspoon ground cloves
1 cup brown sugar, packed	½ teaspoon nutmeg
1 egg, unbeaten	1 teaspoon ginger
¼ cup light molasses	¼ teaspoon salt
3¼ cups sifted regular all-purpose flour	White or colored sugar
2 teaspoons double-acting baking powder	Chopped nuts
	Flaked coconut
	Cut-up gumdrops

Make up dough day before:
1. In large bowl, with mixer at medium speed, cream shortening with butter; gradually add brown sugar, beating until fluffy. Beat in egg and molasses.
2. Onto wax paper sift flour with baking powder, baking soda, cloves, nutmeg, ginger, and salt. Beat into egg mixture, mixing well.
3. Wrap dough in wax paper; refrigerate overnight.
Early next day:
1. Start heating oven to 350°F.
2. On floured, cloth-covered surface, roll out one-third or one-half of dough at a time, refrigerating rest. For crisp cookies, roll dough paper-thin. For softer cookies, roll ⅛-inch to ¼-inch thick.
3. With floured cutter cut into desired shapes, keeping cuttings close together.
4. With broad spatula, place cookies on greased cookie sheets, ½ inch apart. Sprinkle with sugars, nuts, coconut, or gumdrops.
5. Bake 10 minutes, or until done.
6. Cool on wire racks. Store in tightly-covered container. Makes about 10 dozen.

DANISH TOFFEE COOKIES

3½ cups sifted cake flour	1 large egg, unbeaten
2 teaspoons double-acting baking powder	2 tablespoons very strong coffee
⅔ cup soft butter or margarine	1½ tablespoons dark rum
½ teaspoon salt	½ cup finely-chopped blanched almonds
1 cup granulated sugar	

1. Sift flour with baking powder.
2. Cream butter with salt until light and fluffy, gradually adding sugar. Add egg, then coffee, then rum, beating well after each addition. Blend in flour mixture,

Golden Cookie Cone

then almonds. Refrigerate about 2 hours, or until dough can be easily handled.

3. Start heating oven to 375°F.

4. On floured surface, roll out dough ⅛ inch to ¼ inch thick. Cut with floured 2¼-inch cutter. Place on ungreased cookie sheets.

5. Bake 10 to 12 minutes, or until done. Makes about 4 dozen.

WILLIE MAE'S FILLED OATMEAL COOKIES

1 teaspoon vinegar	¼ teaspoon salt
½ cup milk	1½ cups granulated sugar
1 cup sifted regular all-purpose flour	5 cups uncooked quick-cooking rolled oats
1 teaspoon baking soda	1 cup snipped pitted dates
1 cup soft shortening (part butter)	1 teaspoon lemon juice
	¼ cup water

1. Stir vinegar into milk; set aside.

2. Sift flour with baking soda.

3. Cream shortening with salt until light and fluffy, gradually adding ¾ cup sugar. Blend in half of flour mixture, then milk, then remaining flour mixture. Stir in rolled oats. Refrigerate 4 hours.

4. Meanwhile, for filling, in saucepan combine dates, ¾ cup sugar, lemon juice, and water; bring to boil; set aside to cool.

5. Start heating oven to 350°F.

6. On well-floured surface, roll out dough ⅛ inch thick (roll only one-third of dough at a time, refrigerate rest). Cut with floured 2-inch round cutter. Spread 1 teaspoonful of date mixture on each of half of cookies. Top with remaining cookies. Place on ungreased cookie sheets.

7. Bake 10 to 12 minutes.

8. Cool on wire racks. Makes about 3 dozen.

TAVERN BISCUIT CUTOUTS

2¼ cups sifted regular all-purpose flour	¼ teaspoon nutmeg
1 cup granulated sugar	1 cup butter or margarine
¼ teaspoon mace	3 tablespoons brandy
	1 egg, beaten

1. In medium bowl mix together flour, sugar, mace, and nutmeg. With pastry blender or two knives, cut in butter until like coarse corn meal; add brandy, knead lightly together. Refrigerate until well chilled.

2. Start heating oven to 350°F.

3. On floured surface, roll out dough to about ⅛-inch thickness. With cookie cutters, cut dough into desired shapes. Place on greased cookie sheets; brush with beaten egg. (Refrigerate dough between rollings.)

4. Bake 10 to 15 minutes, or until golden.

5. With spatula remove cookies to wire racks to cool. Makes about 4 dozen.

Shape-and-Bake Cookies

These cookies are sometimes called "molded" cookies because they are pressed into a mold, or molded into shape by hand. They can also be shaped by using a cookie press or a pastry bag and tube. To mold well, the dough should be only moderately stiff at room temperature. The dough need only be stiff enough to retain the imprint of the mold or hold its shape when baked.

SCANDINAVIAN SPRITZ COOKIES

2 cups sifted regular all-purpose flour	1 cup soft butter or margarine
1 teaspoon double-acting baking powder	¾ cup granulated sugar
⅛ teaspoon salt	1 egg yolk, unbeaten
	1 teaspoon almond extract

Make, then freeze, as follows:

1. Sift flour with baking powder and salt.

2. In large bowl, with mixer at medium speed, beat butter until very soft; gradually beat in sugar, until *very light and fluffy*. Add egg yolk and almond extract, beating until well blended.

3. With mixer at low speed, gradually add flour mixture, beating just until blended. Wrap dough in wax paper. Refrigerate until firm—about 30 minutes.

4. Start heating oven to 350°F.

5. Onto cold, ungreased cookie sheet, with cookie press and star-shaped disk, press out dough in long, straight strips. Cut each strip into 3- or 4-inch pieces; form into S, O, I, and U (or other desired shapes).

6. Bake 8 to 10 minutes, or until edges are golden.

7. Cool on wire racks. Pack cookies in freezer containers with 2 sheets of wax paper between layers, then freeze.

To serve:

Let wrapped cookies stand at room temperature until thawed—about 15 minutes. Then unwrap and serve Makes about 7 dozen.

FINNISH SHORTBREAD

4¼ cups sifted regular all-
   purpose flour
1 cup granulated sugar
Pinch salt
2 cups butter or margarine
½ cup granulated sugar
¾ cup coarsely-chopped
   blanched almonds
1 egg, beaten

Make 2 or 3 weeks ahead, if desired:
1. In large bowl combine flour, 1 cup sugar, and salt. With pastry blender or two knives, cut in butter until like corn meal; then knead until firm. Refrigerate 1 hour.
2. Start heating oven to 375°F.
3. On lightly floured surface, with palms of hands, roll dough into pencil-shaped rolls ½ inch thick; cut rolls into 2-inch pieces.
4. Combine ½ cup sugar and almonds. Now dip top of each 2-inch piece in egg, then in sugar-almond mixture. Place, nut side up, on lightly greased cookie sheets.
5. Bake 12 to 15 minutes, or until light golden.
6. Cool on wire racks. Store in tightly-covered container; these keep well. Makes about 70.

VANILLA RINGS

4¼ cups sifted regular all-
   purpose flour
1 cup granulated sugar
1 cup finely-chopped,
   blanched almonds
1½ cups butter or
   margarine
1 egg, beaten
1 tablespoon vanilla extract

Make 2 or 3 weeks ahead, if desired:
1. In large bowl combine flour, sugar, and almonds. With pastry blender or two knives, cut in butter until like corn meal. Add egg and vanilla; mix well, then knead dough until smooth. Refrigerate 1 hour.
2. Start heating oven to 375°F.
3. On lightly floured surface, with cookie press and star-shaped disk, press out dough in long, straight strips. Cut each strip into 4-inch pieces; shape each piece into a ring or a letter S. Place on lightly greased cookie sheets.
4. Bake 12 to 15 minutes, or until light golden around edges.
5. Remove to wire racks; cool. Store in tightly-covered container; these keep very well. Makes about 98.

SCOTCH FANS
(Pictured on page 12)

1 cup butter or margarine
½ teaspoon salt
¾ cup light-brown sugar,
   firmly packed
2¼ to 2½ cups sifted
   regular all-purpose flour

Make a few days ahead:
1. In large bowl, with mixer at medium speed, blend

butter with salt. Gradually add brown sugar while beating until smooth and creamy. At low speed, gradually add enough flour to form a stiff dough. Divide dough into 4 parts. Shape each into a ball.
2. Start heating oven to 300°F.
3. Place 2 balls on ungreased cookie sheet; pat into rounds ¼ inch thick. With tines of fork score edges of each round. Then, with fork tines, prick outline of 12 pie-shaped wedges on each round.
4. Bake about 30 to 35 minutes, or until light golden brown.
5. Repeat with remaining 2 balls of dough. While cookies are still warm, cut along fork pricks, but not all the way through. Cool; break into wedges. Makes about 4 dozen.

PECAN FINGERS
(Pictured opposite)

2¼ cups sifted regular all-
   purpose flour
½ teaspoon double-acting
   baking powder
Dash salt
1 cup soft butter or
   margarine
¾ cup granulated sugar
1 egg, unbeaten
1 teaspoon almond extract
1 egg white, slightly beaten
1½ cups chopped pecans

Make at least a day ahead:
1. Sift flour with baking powder and salt.
2. In bowl, with mixer at medium speed, beat butter with sugar until light and fluffy. Beat in egg and almond extract. Gradually add flour mixture, beating until well blended.
3. Start heating oven to 400°F.
4. Onto ungreased cookie sheets, with cookie press and star-shaped disk, press out dough into 3-inch strips. Brush with egg white; sprinkle with pecans. Repeat until all dough is used.
5. Bake 9 to 11 minutes, or until lightly browned at edges.
6. With broad spatula remove to wire racks to cool. Store in tightly-covered container. Makes 5 dozen.

SWEDISH NUT CRESCENTS

1 cup chopped pecans
1¼ cups granulated sugar
1⅓ cups sifted regular all-
   purpose flour
1 teaspoon double-acting
   baking powder
2 teaspoons salt
¼ cup soft shortening
1 egg, unbeaten
2 tablespoons milk
1 teaspoon vanilla extract

1. Start heating oven to 325°F.
2. Combine nuts with ½ cup sugar. Sift flour with baking powder and salt. With mixer at medium speed, beat shortening with ¾ cup sugar, egg, milk, and vanilla until creamy; beat in flour mixture.

Pecan Fingers

3. On greased, inverted 9-by-9-by-2-inch cake pan, spread ¼ cup dough thinly and evenly, sprinkle with 3 tablespoons nut mixture.

4. Bake 10 to 12 minutes, or until golden. At once, while hot, with 1-inch wide spatula, cut into 4½-by-1-inch strips. With spatula, carefully remove strips, one by one, and lay over rolling pin to curve a bit; then remove to wire rack. Repeat, one pan at a time, until all dough is used. Makes about 70.

HALF-MOONS
(Pictured on page 47)

½ cup soft shortening
½ cup soft butter or margarine
⅓ cup granulated sugar
⅔ cup ground blanched almonds

1⅔ cups sifted regular all-purpose flour
¼ teaspoon salt
¼ cup confectioners' sugar
½ teaspoon cinnamon

Make, then freeze this dough:

1. In large bowl, with mixer at high speed, cream shortening with butter and granulated sugar until very light and fluffy. Stir in almonds. Combine flour with salt; stir into shortening mixture.

2. Freezer-wrap and freeze dough until needed (up to one week).

To bake:

1. Unwrap frozen dough; let thaw at room temperature until firm, but pliable.

2. Start heating oven to 325°F.

3. On wax paper, lightly floured if needed, with hands roll a small portion of dough (refrigerate rest) into a roll ½ inch thick; cut it into 4-inch lengths. Then, with fingers, shape each length into a crescent. Place on ungreased cookie sheets.

4. Bake about 10 minutes, or until set, but not brown.

5. Remove very carefully, while hot, and sprinkle with confectioners' sugar combined with cinnamon; let cool on wire racks.

6. Repeat with rest of dough. Store in tightly-covered container. Makes about 4 dozen.

SEMISWEET CRESCENTS
(Pictured on page 47)

½ cup semisweet-chocolate pieces
1 tablespoon milk
2 cups sifted regular all-purpose flour
½ teaspoon salt

¾ cup butter or margarine
½ cup granulated sugar
2 teaspoons vanilla extract
½ cup chopped blanched almonds

Make any time up to 2 weeks ahead:

1. In small saucepan, over hot, *not boiling*, water, melt chocolate pieces with milk; cool slightly.

2. Sift flour with salt.

3. Start heating oven to 350°F.

4. In medium bowl, with mixer at medium speed, beat butter until creamy; beat in sugar and vanilla until light and fluffy; add melted chocolate. Beat in flour mixture gradually until thoroughly blended. Stir in almonds.

5. Shape rounded teaspoons of mixture into crescents; place on ungreased cookie sheets.

6. Bake 12 to 15 minutes.

7. Cool on wire racks. Store in tightly-covered container. Makes 3 dozen.

TEATIME TASSIES

1 3-ounce package soft cream cheese
½ cup soft butter or margarine
1 cup sifted regular all-purpose flour
1 tablespoon butter or margarine

1 egg, unbeaten
¾ cup brown sugar, firmly packed
1 teaspoon vanilla extract
Dash salt
⅔ cup coarsely-broken pecans

Make day before:

1. In bowl, with spoon, thoroughly blend cream cheese with ½ cup butter; then stir in flour. Refrigerate dough about 1 hour.

2. Start heating oven to 325°F.

3. Shape dough into 24 1¾-inch balls. Place one in each cup of greased muffin pans. Press dough to bottom and sides of each cup, as a smooth lining.

4. In small bowl, with mixer at medium speed, beat together 1 tablespoon butter, egg, brown sugar, vanilla, and salt until smooth.

5. Divide pecans in half. Use half to sprinkle on bottom of pastry-lined muffin-pan cups; fill each with about 1 teaspoon egg mixture; top with rest of pecans.

6. Bake 25 minutes.

7. Cool, then carefully remove from pans. Makes 2 dozen.

BANKETLETTER
(Pictured on page 39)

1 cup sifted cake flour
½ teaspoon salt
½ cup butter or margarine
2½ tablespoons ice water

1¼ pounds (2 cups) canned almond paste
½ cup granulated sugar
1 egg, well beaten
¼ teaspoon lemon extract

Make 2 or 3 days ahead:

1. Into bowl sift flour with salt. With pastry blender or two knives, cut in butter until like peas. Gradually, with fork, work in ice water to make dough; refrigerate 1 hour.

2. Meanwhile, in bowl, mix almond paste, sugar, egg, and lemon extract.

3. Start heating oven to 425°F.

4. On lightly-floured surface, roll pastry into 12-inch square; cut into 3 strips, each 4 inches wide. Shape almond-paste mixture into 3 equal rolls, 12 inches by ¾ inch. Place a roll on each pastry strip; fold pastry around it; press seams and ends firmly.

5. On greased cookie sheet, use rolls to form a large family initial. Place rolls seam side down; brush ends with beaten egg before joining.

6. Bake 20 to 25 minutes, or until light golden.

7. Let cool on cookie sheet. Place in foil-lined box and gift-wrap, if desired.

To vary: Make smaller initials as follows: In step 4, above, cut 12-inch square into 6 equal strips; halve crosswise. Shape almond paste into 12 rolls, each 6 inches by ½ inch. Bake as directed. Makes 4 initials.

ALMOND COOKIE PRETZELS
(Pictured on page 47)

1 cup butter or margarine
1 cup sifted confectioners'
  sugar
1 egg yolk, unbeaten
2 eggs, unbeaten
½ teaspoon almond extract
¼ cup commercial sour
  cream

2½ cups instant-type flour*
1 teaspoon double-acting
  baking powder
1 egg yolk mixed with a
  little water
⅓ cup chopped blanched
  almonds

Make any time up to 1 week ahead:

1. In medium bowl, with mixer at medium speed, beat butter until soft. Gradually add sugar, while beating until light and creamy. Beat in egg yolk, eggs, almond extract, and sour cream.

2. On wax paper combine flour and baking powder. Beat into butter mixture, at low speed, until well blended.

3. Start heating oven to 350°F.

4. On well-floured surface, with fingers, shape rounded tablespoons of dough into 10-inch to 12-inch rolls. On ungreased cookie sheets shape each roll into pretzel. Brush with egg yolk-water mixture; sprinkle with nuts.

5. Bake 15 to 20 minutes.

6. Cool on wire rack. Store in tightly-covered container. Makes about 2 dozen.

*Do not sift this flour.

PRETZEL COOKIES

2½ cups sifted regular all-
  purpose flour
2 teaspoons double-acting
  baking powder
10 tablespoons granulated
  sugar
2 teaspoons orange juice
  or vanilla extract

2 tablespoons grated
  orange peel (optional)
3 egg yolks, unbeaten
3 tablespoons milk
6 tablespoons cold butter
  or margarine
½ recipe for Icing, page 27
Orange decorating sugar

Make early on day:

1. Into large mixing bowl sift flour with baking powder and sugar. Add orange juice and peel, egg yolks, and milk. Gradually work into flour mixture until like corn meal.

2. Cut butter into small pieces; place on top of dough; then knead in with hands until dough is very smooth.

3. Wrap dough in wax paper, foil, or saran. Refrigerate about 1 hour, or until chilled.

4. Start heating oven to 400°F.

5. Cut off a piece of dough; with palms of hands roll it into a long thin roll, 12 inches by ½ inch; twist into pretzel shape. Place on lightly greased cookie sheet. Repeat with rest of dough.

6. Bake 10 to 12 minutes, or until firm.

7. Cool on wire rack. When cool, frost with Icing; then sprinkle with decorating sugar. Makes 15.

SMALL PRETZELS

4 cups sifted regular all-
  purpose flour
1 teaspoon cream of tartar
1½ cups butter or
  margarine

1 cup light cream
1 egg, beaten
½ cup granulated sugar

Make 2 or 3 weeks ahead, if desired:

1. In large bowl combine flour with cream of tartar. With pastry blender or two knives, cut in butter until like corn meal. Add cream, a little at a time; blend well. Refrigerate 1 hour.

2. Start heating oven to 400°F.

3. On lightly-floured surface, with palms of hands, roll dough into several pencil-shaped rolls ¼ inch thick; then cut each roll into pieces 8½ inches long. Shape each piece into a pretzel; then dip in egg, then into sugar. Place, coated side up, on lightly greased cookie sheets.

4. Bake 20 minutes, or until light golden.

5. Remove to wire rack; cool. Store in tightly-covered container; these keep well. Makes about 45.

Almond Cookie Tower

CHRISTMAS WREATHS

1 recipe dough for Small
   Pretzels, page 35
Green food color

1 egg white, lightly beaten
Granulated sugar

1. Make dough as directed. Divide into halves. With few drops food color, tint one half a delicate green. Refrigerate both doughs 1 hour.
2. Start heating oven to 400°F.
3. On lightly floured surface, with palms of hands, roll each half of dough into several pencil-shaped rolls ¼ inch thick; cut each roll into pieces about 8½ inches long. Twist one green and one uncolored piece of dough together; shape into a wreathlike ring; pinch ends together. Dip just the top of each wreath into egg white, then into sugar. Place, coated side up, on greased cookie sheets. Repeat with remaining pieces of dough until all are used.
4. Bake 20 minutes, or until light golden.
5. Remove to wire rack; cool. Store in tightly-covered container; these keep well. Makes about 25.

ALMOND COOKIE TOWER
(Pictured opposite)

3 pounds canned almond
   paste
4 egg whites, unbeaten

Confectioners' sugar
Decorating Icing, below

Make a week ahead, or day before, if desired:
1. In large, heavy saucepan, with wooden spoon, mix almond paste with egg whites until well blended. Over low heat, heat about 2 to 3 minutes, or until lukewarm and smooth, kneading with spoon.
2. Turn into bowl. With palms of hands, from some of almond-paste mixture, form a cone-shaped top for the tower, 3 inches high, 1¼ inches wide; set, top side up, on greased cookie sheet.
3. Start heating oven to 300°F.
4. On confectioners'-sugar-covered surface, with palms of hands, roll remaining almond-paste mixture into 12 pencil-shaped rolls, all ½-inch thick and in lengths of 5, 6, 7, 8, 10, 12, 14, 16, 18, 20, 22, and 24 inches.
5. Now, on cookie sheets, shape each roll into a ring, pinching ends together. Starting at base of each ring, gently press ring between thumb and forefinger as you move upward, so it tapers to a sharp crease at top.
6. Measure, and if necessary, reshape rings into these diameters: 2, 2½, 3, 3½, 4, 4½, 5, 5½, 6, 6½, 7, and 7½ inches.
7. Bake 20 to 25 minutes, or until light golden.
8. Cool on cookie sheets. Then, with decorating bag and tube number 4, use Decorating Icing to make zig-zag lines around each ring, from outside to inside; then decorate cone-shaped top. Let dry. Store in tightly-covered container.

Just before serving:
On large serving dish, stack rings starting ⟨ 7½-inch one and graduating up to narrowest one. with cone-shaped piece, as pictured. Garnish as desir⟨ In serving, give each person one of smaller rings, or a piece of a larger one. Makes 8 servings.
DECORATING ICING: Into 2 egg whites, in bowl, gradually stir 4 cups sifted confectioners' sugar until mixture is smooth; cover with wax paper until ready to decorate cookies.

DUTCH ST. NICHOLAS COOKIE
(Pictured on page 39)

1 cup dark-brown sugar
3 tablespoons milk
3 cups sifted regular all-
   purpose flour
1½ teaspoons ground
   cloves
1½ teaspoons cinnamon
¾ teaspoon ginger

¾ teaspoon nutmeg
⅛ teaspoon double-acting
   baking powder
⅛ teaspoon salt
1¼ cups butter or
   margarine
¼ cup slivered blanched
   almonds

Make dough day before:
1. In small bowl, combine brown sugar and milk; stir until smooth.
2. Into large bowl sift flour with cloves, cinnamon, ginger, nutmeg, baking powder, and salt. With pastry blender or two knives, cut in butter until mixture is like corn meal.
3. Add sugar mixture and almonds; mix well. Wrap dough in foil, saran, or wax paper and refrigerate until needed.
At baking time:
1. Brush carvings in large wooden mold well with small brush; do not wash; then dust every nook and cranny well with flour.
2. Start heating oven to 350°F.
3. Press enough dough into mold to *completely* fill it; then, with small knife, cut around edge of pattern, removing trimmings.
4. Invert lightly-greased cookie sheet over mold, then turn both together until mold is on top; tap lightly until dough slips out onto cookie sheet.
5. Bake 20 to 30 minutes, or until light brown.
6. Cool on cookie sheet; then wrap carefully in foil or saran until serving time.
If using small wooden molds:
1. Prepare dough as directed.
2. Fill small molds completely; trim off any excess. Invert mold on floured surface; tap to release cookie. Place, pattern side up, on lightly-greased cookie sheet. Repeat.
3. Bake at 350°F. 15 minutes, or until light brown.
4. Remove to wire rack to cool. Store in tightly-covered container; these keep well.

...ling pin:
...s directed.
...ith ...ed surface, roll out some of dough
...stamp it with patterned rolling pin.
Top ...ace on lightly-greased cookie sheets.
d. 37

... 15 minutes, or until golden.
...acks. Makes about 98.

GINGERBREAD MEN

1 cup granulated sugar	½ teaspoon salt
½ cup soft shortening	1 teaspoon ginger
1 cup dark molasses	1 teaspoon cinnamon
1 teaspoon baking soda	½ teaspoon nutmeg
1 cup buttermilk	1 egg white, beaten
About 6 cups sifted regular all-purpose flour	Raisins

Make about 1 week ahead:

1. In medium bowl, with mixer at medium speed, blend sugar with shortening, then with molasses, until light and fluffy. Dissolve baking soda in buttermilk, then add to molasses mixture.
2. Sift 3 cups flour with salt, ginger, cinnamon, and nutmeg. Blend into molasses mixture; then add enough more flour to make a stiff dough.
3. Lightly press enough dough into a wooden gingerbread-man mold to fill the design, then use rolling pin to flatten surface.* Turn out onto ungreased cookie sheet and trim off edges. Repeat until all of dough is used. Refrigerate on cookie sheet until gingerbread men are firm.
4. Start heating oven to 375°F.
5. Brush firm gingerbread men with beaten egg white. Press on raisins for eyes and buttons.
6. Bake about 10 minutes, or until done.
7. Cool on wire racks. Store in tightly-covered container. Makes 10 cookies (in 8½ by 3-inch mold).
*If wooden gingerbread-man mold is not available, shape dough into balls, then roll out, on floured cloth-covered surface, to ⅛-inch thickness. Cut into desired shapes with favorite cookie cutters. Bake as directed above.

BRAZIL-NUT SNOWBALLS
(Pictured on page 12)

¾ cup butter or margarine	½ teaspoon salt
½ cup granulated sugar	2 cups finely-ground Brazil nuts
1 egg, unbeaten	
2 teaspoons vanilla extract	Confectioners' sugar
2 cups sifted regular all-purpose flour	

Make several days ahead:

1. In large bowl, with mixer at medium speed, beat butter with sugar until creamy. Beat in egg and vanilla and continue beating until mixture is fluffy.
2. Start heating oven to 350°F.
3. Sift flour with salt. Add to butter mixture with Brazil nuts; beat in thoroughly.
4. Shape into ⅔-inch balls. Place on ungreased cookie sheets.
5. Bake 20 minutes.
6. Cool slightly on cookie sheets; roll in confectioners' sugar. Makes about 7 dozen.

CHOCOLATE-ALMOND BUTTERBALLS

⅓ cup semisweet-chocolate pieces	2 teaspoons vanilla extract
1 tablespoon milk	2 cups sifted regular all-purpose flour
¾ cup soft butter or margarine	½ cup chopped blanched almonds
½ teaspoon salt	Granulated sugar
½ cup granulated sugar	

1. Start heating oven to 350°F.
2. Melt chocolate with milk over hot, *not boiling,* water; cool.
3. Meanwhile, cream butter with salt until light and fluffy, gradually adding ½ cup sugar. Blend in vanilla and cooled chocolate mixture. Mix in flour, then almonds until well blended.
4. Shape dough into 1-inch balls. Roll in granulated sugar. Place on ungreased cookie sheets.
5. Bake 12 to 15 minutes. Cool on wire racks. Makes about 3½ dozen.

BLACK AND WHITE SNOWBALLS

2 cups sifted regular all-purpose flour	1 cup pecans, chopped
½ teaspoon salt	1 6-ounce package (1 cup) semisweet-chocolate pieces
¾ cup butter or margarine	
½ cup granulated sugar	Confectioners' sugar
1 egg, unbeaten	Chocolate-milk-flavored mix
2 teaspoons vanilla extract	

Make any time up to 1 week ahead:

1. Onto wax paper sift flour with salt.
2. In large bowl, with mixer at medium speed, cream butter; gradually beat in granulated sugar, beating until light and fluffy.
3. Start heating oven to 350°F.
4. Into sugar mixture beat egg and vanilla; then beat in flour mixture. Stir in pecans and chocolate pieces.
5. Shape into 1-inch balls. Place on ungreased cookie sheets.
6. Bake 15 to 20 minutes.
7. Cool slightly, then roll half of balls in confectioners' sugar, other half in chocolate-milk-flavored mix. Store in tightly-covered container. Makes about 5 dozen.

Dutch St. Nicholas Cookie, Banketletter

To freeze Black and White Snowballs: Make cookies as directed on page 38, then freezer-wrap and freeze up to 2 months. To serve, thaw, unwrapped, at room temperature about 15 minutes.

THUMBPRINTS

½ cup soft butter or margarine	2 tablespoons milk
½ teaspoon salt	¼ cup semisweet-chocolate pieces, chopped
1 teaspoon vanilla extract	Sifted confectioners' sugar
½ cup brown sugar, packed	Chocolate Filling, below
1½ cups sifted regular all-purpose flour	

1. Start heating oven to 375°F.
2. Mix butter, salt, vanilla, and brown sugar until light and fluffy. Blend in flour, milk, and chocolate pieces.
3. Shape into 1-inch balls. Place on ungreased cookie sheets. With thumb make depression in center top of each cookie.
4. Bake 10 to 20 minutes.
5. Immediately roll cookies in confectioners' sugar; cool on wire rack. Meanwhile, make Chocolate Filling. Heap filling in thumbprint depression in top centers of cookies. Makes 3 dozen.

CHOCOLATE FILLING: Over hot, *not boiling,* water, melt ¾ cup semisweet-chocolate pieces with 1 tablespoon shortening, stirring. Cool slightly; add 2 tablespoons corn syrup, 1 tablespoon water, and 1 teaspoon vanilla extract.

FUDGE-NUT MOUNDS

⅔ cup butter or margarine	1 teaspoon double-acting baking powder
1⅔ cups granulated sugar	½ teaspoon salt
1 8-ounce package creamed cottage cheese, sieved	½ cup semisweet-chocolate pieces
2 eggs, unbeaten	½ cup coarsely-chopped walnuts
2 teaspoons vanilla extract	Confectioners' sugar
2¾ cups sifted regular all-purpose flour	Finely chopped walnuts
½ cup Dutch process cocoa	

Make, then freeze, as follows:
1. In large bowl, with mixer at medium speed, beat butter with granulated sugar until light and fluffy; beat in cottage cheese, then eggs and vanilla.
2. Sift flour with cocoa, baking powder, and salt; with mixer at low speed, beat flour mixture into butter-sugar mixture; add chocolate pieces and coarsely-chopped walnuts.
3. Divide dough into 3 portions; wrap each portion in foil or saran, then refrigerate several hours or until firm.
4. Start heating oven to 350°F.

5. Shape dough into 1¼-inch balls. Roll some in confectioners' sugar, some in granulated sugar and some in walnuts. Place on greased cookie sheets.
6. Bake 15 minutes.
7. Cool on wire racks. Freezer-wrap cookies—some of each type—in several packages; freeze.
To serve:
Let cookies stand at room temperature, fully wrapped, until thawed—about 1 hour, then unwrap. Makes about 6 dozen.

CHOCOLATE CRACKLE-TOPS
(Pictured on page 12)

2 eggs, unbeaten	¼ cup packaged dried bread crumbs
1 cup granulated sugar	2 tablespoons regular all-purpose flour
3 squares unsweetened chocolate, finely grated	½ teaspoon cinnamon
2 cups pecans, finely ground	½ teaspoon ground cloves
	Confectioners' sugar

Make several days before:
1. In large bowl, with mixer at medium speed, beat eggs with granulated sugar until well blended. With large wooden spoon, stir in chocolate, pecans, bread crumbs, flour, cinnamon, and cloves, mixing well. Refrigerate about 15 minutes.
2. Start heating oven to 325°F.
3. With a teaspoon and fingers, shape enough of the dough into 1-inch balls to arrange, 1 inch apart, on greased cookie sheets. Roll each ball on all sides in confectioners' sugar, then place on cookie sheets. (Refrigerate rest of dough.)
4. Bake 12 to 15 minutes—they'll be soft and crackled on top.
5. Remove to wire racks to cool. Repeat with rest of dough. Store in tightly-covered container. Makes about 4 dozen.

COCONUT BUTTERBALLS

1 cup soft butter or margarine	2 cups sifted regular all-purpose flour
¼ cup sifted confectioners' sugar	1½ cups flaked coconut
1 teaspoon vanilla extract	Sifted confectioners' sugar

1. Cream butter until light and fluffy, gradually adding sugar, then vanilla. Blend in flour, then coconut.
2. Shape into 1-inch balls. Place, about 2 inches apart, on ungreased cookie sheets. Refrigerate about 15 minutes.
3. Start heating oven to 350°F.
4. Bake balls 15 minutes, or until delicately browned.
5. While cookies are still warm, roll each in sifted confectioners' sugar. Makes about 4 dozen.

ENGLISH TEACAKES

1¾ cups sifted regular all-
   purpose flour
1½ teaspoons double-acting
   baking powder
¼ teaspoon salt
¼ cup soft shortening
¼ cup soft butter or
   margarine

¾ cup granulated sugar
1 egg, unbeaten
3 tablespoons milk
½ cup chopped citron
½ cup currants or raisins
1 egg white, slightly beaten
Granulated sugar

1. Sift flour with baking powder and salt.
2. In large bowl, with mixer at medium speed, mix shortening, butter, sugar, and egg until creamy. Add milk, citron, currants, and flour mixture; mix well. Refrigerate.
3. Start heating oven to 400°F.
4. Roll dough into balls the size of walnuts. Dip tops in egg white, then sugar. Place, sugared sides up, 2 inches apart, on greased cookie sheet.
5. Bake 12 to 15 minutes, or until golden.
6. Cool on wire rack; store. These keep well. Makes about 3 dozen.

HIDDEN TREASURES

½ cup soft shortening
½ cup soft butter or
   margarine
1½ cups granulated sugar
2 eggs, unbeaten
3 cups sifted regular
   all-purpose flour
1 teaspoon double-acting
   baking powder

1 teaspoon cream of tartar
1½ cups walnuts, finely
   chopped
1 cup fresh cranberries,
   snipped
¼ cup dry vermouth
Granulated sugar
Walnut halves

Make any time up to 2 weeks ahead:
1. Day before baking, in large bowl, with mixer at medium speed, beat shortening with butter and 1½ cups sugar until creamy. Beat in eggs, one at a time, beating well after each addition.

2. Into second bowl sift flour with baking powder and cream of tartar; add chopped walnuts and cranberries and toss together until nuts and cranberries are well coated with flour. Stir into shortening mixture with vermouth.
3. Wrap dough securely in wax paper or foil; refrigerate overnight.
On baking day:
1. Start heating oven to 400°F.
2. Form bits of chilled cookie dough into 1-inch balls; roll in granulated sugar. Place, about 2 inches apart, on greased cookie sheets. Place a walnut half in center of each ball, pressing gently to anchor it, but not flatten cookie.
3. Bake 10 minutes.
4. Remove at once from cookie sheets; cool on wire racks. Store in tightly-covered container. Makes about 9 dozen.

CINNAMON CRISPS

1¼ cups sifted regular all-
   purpose flour
1 teaspoon double-acting
   baking powder
¼ teaspoon salt
½ cup soft butter or
   margarine

1 cup granulated sugar
1 egg, unbeaten
1 teaspoon vanilla extract
½ cup finely-chopped
   walnuts
2 teaspoons cinnamon

Make any time up to 1 week ahead:
1. Sift flour with baking powder and salt.
2. In small bowl, with mixer at medium speed, cream butter with sugar, egg, and vanilla until light and fluffy. Add flour mixture gradually, beating until smooth and blended. Refrigerate 1 hour.
3. Start heating oven to 375°F.
4. Shape chilled dough into balls, 1 heaping teaspoon to each. Roll each ball in combined nuts and cinnamon. Place on greased cookie sheet, 2 inches apart.
5. Bake 12 to 15 minutes, or until done.
6. Cool on wire racks. Store in loosely-covered container. Makes 3 dozen.

KING-SIZE GINGERSNAPS

2 cups sifted regular all-
   purpose flour
½ teaspoon salt
1 teaspoon ground cloves
1 teaspoon ginger
1 teaspoon cinnamon
3 teaspoons baking soda

¾ cup soft vegetable
   shortening
1 cup granulated sugar
1 egg, slightly beaten
¼ cup light molasses
Granulated sugar

1. Start heating oven to 350°F.
2. Sift flour with salt, cloves, ginger, cinnamon, and baking soda.
3. In large bowl, with mixer at medium speed, cream

shortening until light and fluffy, gradually adding sugar. Blend in egg and molasses; stir in flour mixture until well blended.

4. Shape dough into 1½-inch balls; roll in granulated sugar. Place, 3 inches apart, on ungreased cookie sheets. Flatten with fingers; sprinkle with more sugar.

5. Bake 8 to 10 minutes.

6. Let stand a minute before removing to wire racks to cool. Store in tightly-covered container; these keep wonderfully well. Makes 18.

CRINKLES

2¼ cups sifted regular all-purpose flour	1 teaspoon ginger
1 teaspoon salt	¾ cup soft shortening
2 teaspoons baking soda	1 cup brown sugar, packed
1 teaspoon cinnamon	1 egg, unbeaten
½ teaspoon ground cloves	¼ cup molasses
	Granulated sugar

1. Sift flour with salt, baking soda, cinnamon, cloves, and ginger.

2. In large bowl, with mixer at medium speed, mix shortening with brown sugar and egg until very light and fluffy. Mix in molasses, then flour mixture. Refrigerate 1 hour or longer.

3. Start heating oven to 375°F.

4. Shape dough into walnut-size balls; dip one side of each into granulated sugar. Place, sugar side up, 3 inches apart, on greased cookie sheets. Sprinkle each cookie with 2 or 3 drops of water.

5. Bake 12 to 15 minutes, or until done. Makes 4 to 5 dozen.

PUMPKINS: Before sprinkling cookies with water, flatten each ball with fork. Press a bit of citron into top, for stem. Bake as above.

CINNAMON-GINGER WAFERS
(Pictured on page 12)

¾ cup molasses	2 cups sifted regular all-purpose flour
6 tablespoons butter or margarine	⅛ teaspoon baking soda
⅓ cup granulated sugar	¼ teaspoon salt
1 egg yolk, unbeaten	1¼ teaspoons ginger
	1¼ teaspoons cinnamon

Make day before:

1. In 2-quart saucepan heat molasses, but *do not boil.* Add butter and stir until melted. With large wooden spoon beat in sugar, then remove from heat and cool 5 minutes.

2. With spoon, beat in egg yolk.

3. Sift flour with baking soda, salt, ginger, and cinnamon; stir into molasses mixture; refrigerate, in saucepan, about 1 hour.

4. Start heating oven to 400°F.

5. With fingers and a teaspoon, shape dough into ½-inch balls. Place, about 2½ inches apart, on greased cookie sheets. (Refrigerate rest of dough.) With floured fingers, flatten each of balls into a wafer-thin cookie.

6. Bake 3 to 4 minutes, or until just browned at edges —timing carefully to prevent burning.

7. Remove wafers very carefully to wire racks to cool —they are brittle and break easily. Repeat with rest of dough. Store, uncovered, to keep crispness. Makes about 5 dozen.

NUT CHERRYETTES

¾ cup soft shortening	2 cups sifted regular all-purpose flour
¼ cup soft butter or margarine	1 egg white, beaten
½ cup confectioners' sugar	1½ cups chopped toasted almonds
½ teaspoon salt	About 24 glacéed cherries, halved
2 teaspoons vanilla extract	

Make any time up to 2 weeks ahead:

1. In medium bowl, with mixer at medium speed, beat shortening with butter and sugar until creamy. Add salt, vanilla, and flour; mix well. Refrigerate dough until cold.

2. Start heating oven to 350°F.

3. Shape dough into 1-inch balls; dip in beaten egg white, then in chopped almonds. Place on ungreased cookie sheets; press a cherry half into each.

4. Bake 12 to 15 minutes, or until light brown.

5. Cool on wire racks. Store in tightly-covered container. Makes about 4 dozen.

PFEFFERNUESSE
(Peppernuts)

4 cups sifted regular all-purpose flour	8 ounces citron, coarsely ground
1 teaspoon baking soda	2 tablespoons butter or margarine
½ teaspoon salt	2½ cups very fine granulated sugar
1 tablespoon cinnamon	5 egg yolks, unbeaten
1 teaspoon ground cloves	1½ teaspoons grated lemon peel
1 teaspoon nutmeg	5 egg whites, stiffly beaten
¼ teaspoon black pepper	Glaze, page 43
1 tablespoon ground cardamom	
1 teaspoon anise seeds	
4 ounces candied orange peel, coarsely ground	

Make several days ahead:

1. Sift flour with baking soda, salt, cinnamon, cloves, nutmeg, and pepper. Add cardamom, anise seeds, orange peel, and citron. Toss to coat well with flour.

2. In large bowl, with mixer at high speed, mix butter with granulated sugar, the egg yolks, and lemon peel

until well blended. With spoon, blend in flour mixture; fold in egg whites. Refrigerate 1 hour.

3. With floured hands, shape dough into small balls. Place on ungreased cookie sheets; let stand, uncovered, 12 hours at room temperature.

At baking time:

1. Start heating oven to 350°F.
2. Bake cookies 15 minutes, or until done.
3. Cool on wire racks. Meanwhile, make Glaze. Frost cooled cookies with Glaze, then, if desired, toss in confectioners' sugar. Makes about 83.

GLAZE: Mix 1½ cups sifted confectioners' sugar with about 3 tablespoons milk until smooth and of spreading consistency.

PEANUT PUFFS

¾ cup soft shortening	2¼ cups sifted regular
½ cup peanut butter	all-purpose flour
½ teaspoon salt	¾ cup salted peanuts,
½ cup sifted confectioners'	finely chopped
sugar	Sifted confectioners' sugar
1 teaspoon vanilla extract	

1. Start heating oven to 375°F.
2. Cream shortening with peanut butter and salt until light and fluffy, gradually adding confectioners' sugar. Blend in vanilla, then flour. Stir in peanuts; mix well.
3. Shape dough into small balls. Place on ungreased cookie sheets.
4. Bake 12 minutes, or until golden brown.
5. Roll immediately in confectioners' sugar. If desired, reroll cookies, when cool, in more confectioners' sugar. Makes 4 dozen.

WALNUT BALLS

2 eggs, unbeaten	4½ cups ground walnuts
1 cup granulated sugar	(about 3 8-ounce cans)
	Confectioners' sugar

Make day before:

1. In large bowl, with mixer at medium speed, beat eggs with sugar until thick and lemon-colored. Fold in ground walnuts, blending well.

2. Start heating oven to 350°F.
3. With hands, shape mixture into 1½-inch balls. Place on greased cookie sheet, sprinkle with confectioners' sugar.
4. Bake 15 to 20 minutes, or until a very light brown.
5. Cool on wire rack. Makes about 30.

PECAN PUFFS
(Pictured on page 12)

1 cup vegetable shortening	½ teaspoon salt
½ cup sifted confectioners'	1 teaspoon vanilla extract
sugar	¾ cup finely-chopped
2¼ cups sifted regular all-	pecans
purpose flour	Confectioners' sugar

Early on day:

1. In bowl, cream shortening with ½ cup sugar until fluffy. Then beat in flour, salt, and vanilla. Carefully fold in pecans.
2. Start heating oven to 375°F.
3. Shape dough into 1-inch balls. Place on greased cookie sheets.
4. Bake 10 to 12 minutes, or until golden.
5. Roll immediately in confectioners' sugar; cool on wire racks. Roll again in sugar. Makes 42.

WALNUT-BUTTER BALLS

1½ cups sifted regular all-	2 teaspoons instant coffee
purpose flour	powder
½ cup granulated sugar	1 cup butter or margarine
¼ teaspoon salt	¾ cup chopped walnuts

1. Start heating oven to 300°F.
2. Into medium bowl sift flour with sugar, salt, and instant coffee powder. With pastry blender or two knives, cut butter until size of small peas.
3. Press dough together. Shape into small balls; roll in chopped walnuts. Place, 2 inches apart, on ungreased cookies sheets; flatten with bottom of glass dipped in sugar.
4. Bake about 20 minutes, or until edges are very light brown.
5. Cool slightly; remove to wire racks. Makes about 3 dozen.

44

Bars and Squares

Probably the most popular of all cookies, bar none, (especially with the cook), these are the easiest of all cookies to make. Just whip up the batter, pour it into the pan, pop it into the oven. No messy rolling and cutting, no greasy cookie sheets to wash, no cookies to remove to racks. No wonder they are so popular with the cook! §Most of these recipes call for regular all-purpose flour, but there are several that use cake flour or instant-type flour. Do not substitute. Use the flour specified in the recipe for best results.

APRICOT-WALNUT BARS
(Pictured on page 12)

¾ cup dried apricots	1 cup brown sugar, packed
Water	½ teaspoon double-acting
1⅓ cups sifted regular all-purpose flour	baking powder
¼ cup granulated sugar	¼ teaspoon salt
½ cup butter or margarine	½ teaspoon vanilla extract
2 eggs, well beaten	½ cup chopped walnuts

Early on day:
1. Rinse apricots. In saucepan, cover apricots with water; bring to boil; then simmer 10 minutes. Drain, cool, and chop.
2. Start heating oven to 325°F.
3. Into bowl sift 1 cup flour with granulated sugar; with pastry blender or two knives, cut in butter until like coarse corn meal. Press into ungreased 9-by-9-by-2-inch baking pan.
4. Bake 25 minutes.
5. Meanwhile, combine eggs and brown sugar; stir in ⅓ cup flour, baking powder, salt, vanilla, walnuts, and apricots until well blended. Spread evenly over baked layer.
6. Bake 35 minutes.
7. Cool in pan—top will be soft. Cut into 16 large squares or 32 bars.

PARTY APRICOT BARS

1 cup dried apricots	¼ teaspoon salt
Water	1 cup brown sugar, packed
1⅓ cups sifted regular all-purpose flour	1 teaspoon almond extract
⅓ cup granulated sugar	2 eggs, well beaten
½ cup uncooked rolled oats	1 cup flaked coconut
½ cup butter or margarine	Flaked coconut or chopped nuts
½ teaspoon double-acting baking powder	

1. In saucepan, cover apricots with water; bring to boil; then simmer 10 minutes. Drain, cool, and cut into small pieces.
2. Start heating oven to 350°F.
3. In bowl combine 1 cup flour with granulated sugar and rolled oats; with pastry blender or two knives, cut in butter until mixture is crumbly. Press evenly into greased 9-by-9-by-2-inch baking pan.
4. Bake 20 minutes.
5. Meanwhile, sift ⅓ cup flour with baking powder and salt. Gradually blend brown sugar with almond extract and eggs. Stir in flour mixture, 1 cup coconut, and apricots. Spread evenly over baked layer; sprinkle with coconut or nuts.
6. Bake 30 minutes.
7. Cool in pan; cut into 24 bars.

BRAZIL-NUT TRIPLE-LAYER BARS

¼ cup soft butter or margarine	½ cup flaked coconut
½ teaspoon salt	1 teaspoon vanilla extract
1 cup sifted regular all-purpose flour	2 tablespoons flour
2 eggs, well beaten	Orange Cookie Frosting, below
¾ cup brown sugar, packed	Coarsely-chopped Brazil nuts
1 cup finely-chopped Brazil nuts	

1. Start heating oven to 375°F.
2. With wooden spoon, thoroughly blend butter with ¼ teaspoon salt and 1 cup flour. With spatula, press mixture evenly into greased 9-by-9-by-2-inch baking pan.
3. Bake 15 minutes.
4. Meanwhile, into eggs, blend brown sugar, finely chopped nuts, ¼ teaspoon salt, coconut, vanilla, and 2 tablespoons flour. Spread evenly over baked layer.
5. Bake 15 minutes.
6. Cool in pan; then frost with Orange Cookie Frosting; sprinkle with coarsely chopped nuts. Cut into 24 bars or diamonds.

ORANGE COOKIE FROSTING: With mixer at medium speed (or with spoon), thoroughly mix ¼ cup soft butter or margarine with dash salt and ½ cup sifted confectioners' sugar until light and fluffy. Add 1¼ cups sifted confectioners' sugar alternately with about 1 tablespoon orange juice, beating until very smooth and of spreading consistency; beat in ½ teaspoon grated orange peel.

BRAZIL-NUT COFFEECAKE BARS

2 cups sifted regular all-purpose flour	½ cup soft butter or margarine
1 teaspoon double-acting baking powder	½ cup soft shortening
1⅓ cups granulated sugar	1 egg, unbeaten
4 teaspoons cinnamon	1 egg yolk, unbeaten
	1 egg white, slightly beaten
	1 cup chopped Brazil nuts

1.   Start heating oven to 350°F.
2.   Into bowl sift flour with baking powder, 1 cup sugar, and 3 teaspoons cinnamon; add butter, shortening, whole egg, and egg yolk. With mixer at low speed (or with spoon), mix well. Turn into ungreased 15½-by-10½-by-1-inch jelly-roll pan; spread evenly with spatula.
3.   Brush dough with slightly beaten egg whites. Combine remaining ⅓ cup sugar, 1 teaspoon cinnamon, and nuts; sprinkle over top of dough.
4.   Bake 25 minutes, or until nuts are golden.
5.   Cool in pan; cut into 75 2-by-1-inch bars.

BUTTERSCOTCH AMBROSIA BARS

¾ cup soft shortening	½ teaspoon double-acting baking powder
1 cup brown sugar, firmly packed	½ teaspoon baking soda
1 egg, unbeaten	¼ cup orange juice
1 tablespoon grated orange peel	1 6-ounce package butterscotch pieces (1 cup)
2 cups instant-type flour*	1 cup flaked coconut
¾ teaspoon salt	

1.   Start heating oven to 350°F.
2.   In bowl, with mixer at medium speed, beat shortening with brown sugar until creamy; then beat in egg and orange peel.
3.   On wax paper combine flour, salt, baking powder, and baking soda. Beat into sugar mixture alternately with orange juice. Stir in butterscotch pieces and coconut. Spread batter evenly in greased 13-by-9-by-2-inch baking dish.
4.   Bake 30 minutes, or until cake tester, inserted in center, comes out clean.
5.   Cool in pan on wire rack; cut into 36 1½-by-1-inch bars. Store, foil-wrapped, at room temperature.
To freeze: Make, bake, and cool bars as directed; freezer-wrap and freeze up to 2 months before using. Thaw, unwrapped, at room temperature about 30 minutes.
*Do not sift this flour.

CASHEW-CARAMEL YUMMIES

¾ cup sifted regular all-purpose flour	½ cup chopped salted cashew nuts
½ teaspoon double-acting baking powder	2 tablespoons melted butter or margarine
¼ teaspoon salt	1½ tablespoons light cream
2 eggs, slightly beaten	⅓ cup chopped salted cashew nuts
½ cup granulated sugar	
¾ cup brown sugar, packed	

1.   Start heating oven to 350°F.
2.   Sift flour with baking powder and salt.
3.   Into slightly beaten eggs, stir granulated sugar and ½ cup brown sugar. Blend in ½ cup nuts and flour mixture. Turn mixture into greased 9-by-9-by-2-inch pan.
3.   Bake 20 to 25 minutes, or until crust springs back when lightly touched with finger.
4.   Meanwhile, make topping: Into butter, stir ¼ cup brown sugar, cream, and ⅓ cup nuts. Spread immediately on baked layer, covering top completely.
5.   Place under broiler about 1 minute, or until topping bubbles and is light brown.
6.   While still warm, cut into 36 bars; cool thoroughly in pan.

LEBKUCHEN

2¼ cups sifted regular all-purpose flour	3 eggs, unbeaten
½ teaspoon salt	1 egg yolk, unbeaten
1 teaspoon double-acting baking powder	1½ cups dark-brown sugar, packed
½ teaspoon ground cloves	½ cup strong coffee or sherry
1 teaspoon cinnamon	1 cup sifted confectioners' sugar
1 cup broken walnuts	2 tablespoons milk
½ pound canned diced mixed preserved fruit	

Make day before:
1.   Sift flour with salt, baking powder, cloves, and cinnamon. Add nuts and fruit, tossing to coat well.
2.   Start heating oven to 375°F.
3.   In large bowl, with mixer at high speed, beat eggs and egg yolk until thick and lemon-colored. Add brown sugar gradually, beating well after each addition.
4.   With spoon, blend in coffee, then flour mixture, until well blended. Turn into greased 15½-by-10½-by-1-inch jelly-roll pan.
5.   Bake 25 minutes, or until cake tester, inserted in center, comes out clean, and top springs back when lightly touched.
6.   Cool in pan; frost with confectioners' sugar combined with milk. Cut into 24 bars. Store in tightly-covered container with half an apple to keep bars soft. Or freeze, if desired.

ORIENTAL CRUNCH

1 cup butter or margarine	2 cups sifted regular all-
2 tablespoons instant	purpose flour
coffee powder	1 6-ounce package
½ teaspoon salt	semisweet-chocolate
½ teaspoon almond extract	pieces (1 cup)
1 teaspoon vanilla extract	½ cup almonds, coarsely
1 cup granulated sugar	chopped

1. Start heating oven to 375°F.
2. Blend butter with instant coffee powder, salt, almond and vanilla extracts. Gradually beat in sugar, then flour; add chocolate pieces. Spread in ungreased 15½-by-10½-by-1-inch jelly-roll pan. Sprinkle almonds over top; press them in.
3. Bake 20 to 22 minutes.
4. Cool in pan, then break into irregular pieces. Makes 1¾ pounds.

COFFEE BROWNIES

¾ cup sifted regular all-	2 squares unsweetened
purpose flour	chocolate
½ teaspoon double-acting	⅓ cup butter or margarine
baking powder	2 eggs, unbeaten
¼ teaspoon salt	1 cup granulated sugar
2 tablespoons instant	1 teaspoon vanilla extract
coffee powder	½ cup chopped walnuts

1. Start heating oven to 375°F.
2. Sift flour with baking powder, salt, and instant coffee powder.
3. In double boiler, over hot, *not boiling*, water, melt chocolate with butter; cool.
4. In medium bowl, beat eggs with sugar until very light and fluffy; add to chocolate mixture; mix until well blended.
5. Stir flour mixture into chocolate mixture until blended; add vanilla and nuts and mix gently. Pour into greased 8-by-8-by-2-inch pan.
6. Bake 25 minutes, or until center springs back when gently pressed with finger.
7. Cool in pan; cut into 16 squares.

DOUBLE-DECK BROWNIES

⅔ cup sifted regular all-	⅓ cup melted butter or
purpose flour	shortening
½ teaspoon double-acting	⅓ cup flaked coconut*
baking powder	½ teaspoon almond extract
¼ teaspoon salt	1½ squares unsweetened
2 eggs, unbeaten	chocolate, melted
1 cup granulated sugar	

1. Start heating oven to 350°F.
2. Sift flour with baking powder and salt.
3. With hand beater, or mixer at medium speed, beat

eggs well, gradually adding sugar. Stir in melted butter, then flour mixture, blending well.
4. Into small bowl, pour one-fourth of batter; blend in coconut and almond extract. Into remaining three-fourths of batter, blend chocolate. Spread this mixture evenly in greased 8-by-8-by-2-inch pan. Onto this carefully spoon coconut batter; spread to form a thin, smooth layer.
5. Bake 35 minutes, or until done.
6. Cool in pan on wire rack; cut into 24 bars or squares.
*If desired, increase coconut to ¾ cup; stir into batter before dividing.

DOUBLE-WALNUT BROWNIE SQUARES
(Pictured on page 54)

1 cup granulated sugar	1 cup sifted regular all-
2 tablespoons soft butter	purpose flour
or margarine	1 teaspoon double-acting
1 egg, unbeaten	baking powder
1 teaspoon vanilla extract	½ cup undiluted
2 envelopes (2 ounces)	evaporated milk
no-melt unsweetened	1¼ cups finely-chopped
chocolate	walnuts

Make early on day:
1. In large bowl, with mixer at medium speed, beat sugar, butter, egg, and vanilla until well blended. Now beat in chocolate.
2. Start heating oven to 350°F.
3. Sift flour with baking powder; beat into sugar mixture alternately with evaporated milk. Stir in 1 cup nuts. Pour into greased 9-by-9-by-2-inch baking dish; sprinkle with rest of nuts.
4. Bake 30 minutes, or until cake tester, inserted in center, comes out clean.
5. Cool in pan on wire rack. Cover with foil; store at room temperature. When ready to serve, cut into 16 squares.

CHOCOLATE DELIGHTS
(Pictured opposite)

½ cup butter or margarine	2 egg whites, unbeaten
3 tablespoons granulated	⅛ teaspoon salt
sugar	¼ cup granulated sugar
2 egg yolks, unbeaten	¼ cup ground blanched
1 teaspoon vanilla extract	almonds
2 cups sifted regular all-	½ cup sliced blanched
purpose flour	almonds
¼ cup semisweet-chocolate	
pieces	

Make a day or two before:
1. Start heating oven to 350°F.
2. In large bowl, with mixer at medium speed, beat

Chocolate Delights, Semisweet Crescents and Half-Moons, Chocolate Bits, Butterscotch Pinwheels, Ting-a-Lings, Almond Cookie Pretzels, Christmas Daisies, Triangles, Marble Curls

butter with 3 tablespoons sugar, egg yolks, and vanilla until fluffy. Gradually add flour, beating until well blended. (Mixture will be crumbly.) Press into greased 9-by-9-by-2-inch cake pan.

3. Bake 20 minutes.

4. Meanwhile, over hot, *not boiling*, water, melt chocolate pieces; cool slightly.

5. In small bowl, beat egg whites with salt until frothy; then gradually beat in ¼ cup sugar until stiff peaks form. Gradually fold in ground almonds and chocolate. Spread evenly over baked layer; sprinkle with sliced almonds.

6. Bake 20 minutes, or until almonds are golden and cake tester comes out clean.

7. Cool in pan; cut into 16 squares. Store, tightly covered, at room temperature.

RASPBERRY-CHOCOLATE DELIGHTS: Prepare as in steps 1 through 4, above. Spread baked layer with ½ cup raspberry jam, then continue as in steps 5 through 7.

CHOCOLATE HALFWAY BARS

1 cup sifted regular all- purpose flour	¼ cup brown sugar, packed
⅛ teaspoon salt	1 egg yolk, unbeaten
⅛ teaspoon baking soda	1½ teaspoons water
½ teaspoon double-acting baking powder	½ teaspoon vanilla extract
½ cup soft shortening	½ cup semisweet-chocolate pieces
¼ cup granulated sugar	1 egg white, unbeaten
	½ cup brown sugar, packed

1. Start heating oven to 375°F.

2. Sift flour with salt, baking soda, and baking powder.

3. Mix shortening, granulated sugar, and ¼ cup brown sugar until *very light and fluffy*. Add egg yolk, water, and vanilla; mix well. Mix in flour thoroughly. Press into greased 12-by-8-by-2-inch baking dish; top with chocolate.

4. Beat egg white until stiff; gradually beat in ½ cup brown sugar. Spread over chocolate.

5. Bake 25 minutes, or until done.

6. While still warm cut into 32 bars; cool in baking dish.

CHOCOLATE CHEWS

2 eggs, slightly beaten	½ cup plus 1 tablespoon
1 cup granulated sugar	sifted regular all-purpose
½ teaspoon vanilla extract	flour
½ cup butter or margarine	½ to 1 cup chopped
2 squares unsweetened	walnuts or pistachios
chocolate	

1. Start heating oven to 350°F.

2. In medium bowl, mix eggs well with sugar, and vanilla.

3. Melt butter with chocolate. Cool a bit; mix with egg mixture. Add flour; mix well. Turn into greased 11-by-7-by-1½-inch baking pan; top with nuts.

4. Bake 35 to 40 minutes, or until done.

5. Cool in pan; cut into 24 squares.

TEA BROWNIES: Use 2 8-by-8-by-2-inch pans. Bake 15 to 20 minutes. Cool in pans; cut with small fancy cookie cutters. Or put layers together with Orange Cookie Frosting, page 44; then cut.

FUDGE CUTS: Bake as for Tea Brownies, above; cut into 32 2-inch squares.

FROSTED FUDGE-NUT THINS

¾ cup sifted regular all- purpose flour	1 cup granulated sugar
1 teaspoon double-acting baking powder	2 eggs, unbeaten
¼ teaspoon salt	½ teaspoon vanilla extract
½ cup butter or margarine	½ cup chopped walnuts

2 squares unsweetened
    chocolate
	Almond Fudge Frosting,
	    below

	½ cup chopped walnuts

Make and freeze dough up to 1 week ahead:

1. Sift flour with baking powder and salt.

2. In medium saucepan, over low heat, melt butter with chocolate, stirring constantly. Remove from heat.

3. Into chocolate mixture blend sugar, eggs, and vanilla, then flour mixture. Stir in ½ cup walnuts and mix thoroughly. Freezer-wrap and freeze until ready to bake.

Early on day:

1. Start heating oven to 375°F.

2. With small spatula spread thawed dough evenly in a 15½-by-10½-by-1-inch jelly-roll pan that has been greased, lined with wax paper and greased again.

3. Bake 17 to 20 minutes, or until cake tester, inserted in center, comes out clean.

4. Meanwhile, make Almond Fudge Frosting. Spread evenly over cooled cookies. Sprinkle top with ½ cup nuts, pressing them in slightly. Cut into 36 bars. Store, tightly covered, until needed.

ALMOND FUDGE FROSTING: In small saucepan melt 1 tablespoon butter with 1 square unsweetened chocolate in ¼ cup water. Remove from heat; add 1½ cups sifted confectioners' sugar and ½ teaspoon almond extract, beating until of spreading consistency.

To freeze baked cookies: Make and bake as above. Freezer-wrap and freeze in pan. On serving day, unwrap, let stand at room temperature until thawed, then frost and cut as above.

CHOCOLATE ORANGE-MARMALADE BARS
(Pictured on page 54)

1½ cups sifted regular all-purpose flour	1½ tablespoons orange marmalade
1½ teaspoons double-acting baking powder	1 tablespoon grated orange peel
¼ teaspoon salt	½ cup orange juice
6 tablespoons butter or margarine	1 cup confectioners' sugar
½ cup granulated sugar	2 tablespoons orange juice
2 eggs, unbeaten	Chocolate sprinkles

Make any time up to 1 week ahead:
1. Sift flour with baking powder and salt.
2. Start heating oven to 350°F.
3. In medium bowl, with mixer at medium speed, beat butter until soft; gradually add granulated sugar, beating until fluffy. Beat in eggs, one at a time; add marmalade and orange peel. Then beat in flour mixture alternately with ½ cup orange juice until blended. Turn into greased 8-by-8-by-2-inch cake pan.
4. Bake 35 to 40 minutes.
5. Cool in pan, then spread with confectioners' sugar mixed with 2 tablespoons orange juice; top with sprinkles. Cut into 12 bars. Store in pan, covered with foil, at room temperature.

SURPRISE BARS

1½ cups sifted regular all-purpose flour	⅔ cup salad oil
1½ teaspoons double-acting baking powder	1 teaspoon vanilla extract
1 teaspoon salt	½ cup chopped walnuts
2 eggs, unbeaten	½ cup semisweet-chocolate pieces
1½ cups light-brown sugar, packed	½ cup butterscotch pieces

1. Start heating oven to 350°F.
2. Onto wax paper sift flour with baking powder and salt.
3. In large bowl, with mixer at high speed, beat eggs until thick and foamy. At medium speed, gradually add sugar; continue to beat until very well blended. Now slowly beat in salad oil and vanilla, mixing well. At low speed, add flour mixture all at once. Fold in nuts and chocolate and butterscotch pieces. With small spatula spread in greased 15½-by-10½-by-1-inch jelly-roll pan.

4. Bake 20 to 25 minutes, or until cake tester, inserted in center, comes out clean.
5. Cool in pan; cut into about 30 bars. Store in covered container.

To freeze: Make and bake as above; then freezer-wrap and freeze. To serve, thaw, unwrapped, at room temperature, about 15 minutes.

CRANBERRY BARS

2 eggs, unbeaten	½ teaspoon salt
1 cup granulated sugar	1 cup pecans, finely chopped
2 teaspoons lemon juice	½ 1-pound can jellied cranberry sauce
1½ cups instant-type flour*	
1½ teaspoons double-acting baking powder	

Make any time up to 1 week ahead:
1. In small bowl, with hand beater, beat eggs with sugar until creamy; add lemon juice and beat until thoroughly blended.
2. Start heating oven to 350°F.
3. On wax paper stir flour, baking powder, and salt together. Stir into egg mixture until well blended; fold in pecans. Cut jellied cranberry sauce into slices ¼-inch thick; then cut slices into small cubes; lightly fold into flour mixture. Turn into greased 13-by-9-by-2-inch baking dish.
4. Bake 30 minutes, or until cake tester, inserted in center, comes out clean.
5. Cool in dish on wire rack; while still slightly warm, cut into 30 bars. Store in baking dish, tightly covered, at room temperature until served.
*Do not sift this flour.

LEMON-GLAZED DATE STICKS

1¼ cups sifted cake flour	1 tablespoon butter or margarine, melted
1¼ teaspoons double-acting baking powder	1 tablespoon hot water
½ teaspoon salt	2 cups finely-cut pitted dates
2 eggs, unbeaten	½ cup coarsely-cut walnuts
1 cup granulated sugar	Lemon Glaze, page 50

1. Start heating oven to 325°F.
2. Sift flour with baking powder and salt.
3. In large bowl, beat eggs well; gradually add sugar. Blend in melted butter and water. Stir in dates and nuts, then add flour mixture gradually, mixing thoroughly. Turn into 2 greased 8-by-8-by-2-inch baking pans.
4. Bake 30 to 35 minutes.
5. Cool in pans. Meanwhile, make Lemon Glaze. Spread top of cooled cookies thinly with glaze; then cut into about 48 small sticks.

LEMON GLAZE: In saucepan heat 3 tablespoons milk with 2 tablespoons butter or margarine. Stir into 2 cups sifted confectioners' sugar until smooth. Blend in 1 teaspoon grated lemon peel and 3 tablespoons lemon juice.

PEACHY BARS

1 16- or 17-ounce can cling-
  peach slices, drained
2 cups seedless raisins
½ cup granulated sugar
¼ cup sifted regular all-
  purpose flour
½ teaspoon nutmeg
1 teaspoon cinnamon
¾ cup undiluted
  evaporated milk
¼ teaspoon almond extract

1 cup brown sugar, packed
1½ teaspoons double-acting
  baking powder
½ teaspoon salt
2 cups sifted regular all-
  purpose flour
¾ cup shortening
⅓ cup undiluted
  evaporated milk
⅓ cup chopped walnuts

Make day before, or early on day:
1. In saucepan combine peaches, raisins, granulated sugar, ¼ cup flour, nutmeg, cinnamon, and ¾ cup un-diluted evaporated milk. Stir gently, over very low heat, until mixture thickens. Cool; stir in almond extract.
2. Start heating oven to 350°F.
3. In large bowl, with pastry blender or two knives, combine brown sugar, baking powder, salt, 2 cups flour, and shortening until like coarse corn meal. Stir in ⅓ cup evaporated milk and walnuts.
4. With fingers, press about three-fourths of brown-sugar mixture into greased 13-by-9-by-2-inch baking dish. With spatula, spread peach mixture over this crust; dot top with remaining brown-sugar mixture.
5. Bake 35 to 40 minutes, or until done.
6. Cool in pan on wire rack. With sharp knife, cut into 24 bars.

ORANGE SAUCEPAN COOKIES
(Pictured on page 12)

½ cup butter or margarine
½ cup granulated sugar
1 teaspoon grated orange
  peel
2 tablespoons orange juice
1 cup sifted regular all-
  purpose flour

½ teaspoon baking soda
1 egg, unbeaten
½ cup chopped walnuts
½ cup chopped pitted dates
Orange Icing, below

Make a few days ahead:
1. In saucepan, melt butter; remove from heat. Add sugar, orange peel and juice; blend.
2. Start heating oven to 350°F.
3. Sift flour with baking soda. Add to butter mixture. Add egg and blend well. Add walnuts and dates; stir lightly to combine. Pour into 9-by-9-by-2-inch cake pan that has been greased on bottom only.

4. Bake about 25 minutes, or until done.
5. Cool in pan. Meanwhile, make Orange Icing. Lightly frost cookies. When set, cut into 16 bars.
ORANGE ICING: With mixer at medium speed, beat 1 tablespoon butter or margarine until soft. Blend in 1 cup sifted confectioners' sugar and 1 tablespoon plus 1 teaspoon orange juice, beating until smooth and of spreading consistency.

NUTTY SQUARES

1 pound prunes
2 eggs, unbeaten
½ cup granulated sugar
½ cup sifted regular all-
  purpose flour
½ teaspoon double-acting
  baking powder

½ teaspoon salt
½ teaspoon vanilla extract
1 cup coarsely-chopped
  walnuts
Confectioners' sugar

Make and freeze any time up to 2 weeks ahead:
1. With kitchen shears, snip flesh from prunes.
2. With mixer at medium speed, beat eggs until foamy; gradually add granulated sugar, beating constantly.
3. Start heating oven to 325°F.
4. Sift flour with baking powder and salt. Add to egg mixture. Stir in vanilla, walnuts, and snipped prunes. Spread in generously greased 8-by-8-by-2-inch baking dish.
5. Bake 40 minutes.
6. While still warm, cut into 16 squares. Cool; freezer-wrap in pan; freeze.
To serve:
Unwrap frozen squares, thaw at room temperature 1½ hours, then sprinkle with confectioners' sugar.

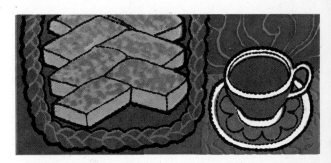

SWEDISH NUT BARS

6 egg yolks, unbeaten
1¼ cups granulated sugar
3½ cups finely-ground
  walnuts

3 teaspoons almond extract
6 egg whites, unbeaten

1. Start heating oven to 325°F.
2. Beat egg yolks until thick and tripled in volume. Add sugar gradually, beating until thick — about 10

minutes. Gently fold in finely-ground walnuts and almond extract.

3. Beat egg whites until stiff but not dry; fold into egg-yolk mixture. Pour into a 9-by-9-by-2-inch cake pan that has been lined with wax paper, then greased.

4. Bake about 1 hour.

5. Cool 10 minutes in pan; turn out; remove paper and let cool completely. Cut as needed (these keep well in refrigerator). Makes about 30.

WALNUT BAR COOKIES

2 egg whites, unbeaten	⅓ cup butter or margarine,
Dash salt	melted and cooled
1 cup brown sugar, packed	2 egg yolks, unbeaten
2 teaspoons vanilla extract	1 cup walnuts, coarsely
½ cup sifted regular all-	chopped
purpose flour	Confectioners' sugar
¼ teaspoon double-acting	
baking powder	

Make any time up to 2 weeks ahead:

1. In small bowl, with mixer at medium speed, beat egg whites with salt until soft peaks form. Beat in brown sugar, ¼ cup at a time, beating well after each addition. Add vanilla.

2. Start heating oven to 350°F.

3. Onto wax paper sift flour with baking powder; sprinkle over egg-white mixture.

4. In small bowl mix butter with egg yolks; pour over flour mixture on egg-white mixture; sprinkle on walnuts. With rubber spatula, fold mixture together just until well mixed. Turn into a 9-by-9-by-2-inch cake pan that has been lined with wax paper, then greased and floured.

5. Bake 25 minutes, or until cake tester, inserted in center, comes out clean.

6. Cool 10 minutes in pan, then cut into 24 2¼-by-1½-inch bars. Dust with confectioners' sugar. Store in cookie jar.

WALNUT SQUARES

½ cup sifted regular all-	1 egg, unbeaten
purpose flour	1 cup brown sugar, packed
½ teaspoon salt	½ teaspoon vanilla extract
⅛ teaspoon baking soda	1 cup chopped walnuts

1. Start heating oven to 325°F.

2. Sift flour with salt and baking soda.

3. With hand beater or mixer, beat egg until foamy. Add brown sugar and vanilla; beat well. Stir in flour mixture, then walnuts. With spatula, spread mixture in well-greased 8-by-8-by-2-inch pan.

4. Bake 25 to 30 minutes, or until top has dull crust.

5. While still warm, cut into 16 2-inch squares; cool completely before removing from pan.

Slice-and-Bake Cookies

Sometimes called icebox or refrigerator cookies, these are made from a stiff dough which is formed into a roll and refrigerated until firm enough to slice easily. The great advantage of many slice-and-bake cookies is that the dough can be made well ahead of time and stored until baking day. Included in this section are some recipes using those wonderful packaged slice 'n' bake refrigerator cookie doughs now available in the dairy case at your supermarket. Watch for them!

PARTY BUTTER COOKIES

¾ cup soft butter or	½ teaspoon vanilla extract
margarine	2 cups sifted cake flour
½ cup granulated sugar	Chocolate Glaze, below
1 egg yolk, unbeaten	

1. Cream butter, gradually adding sugar. Add egg yolk and vanilla; beat well. Gradually blend in flour. Refrigerate about 2 hours, or until easy to handle.

2. Shape into 2 rolls, each 1½ inches in diameter. Wrap each in wax paper or saran; refrigerate overnight or longer.

To bake:

1. Start heating oven to 400°F.

2. Slice dough ⅛ inch thick. Place on ungreased cookie sheets.

3. Bake 8 to 10 minutes, or until edges are golden.

4. Cool; then dip half of top of each cookie into Chocolate Glaze. If desired, while glaze is still soft, sprinkle with chopped nuts, flaked coconut, or chocolate sprinkles. Makes about 6 dozen.

CHOCOLATE GLAZE: Over hot, *not boiling*, water, melt 2 cups semisweet-chocolate pieces; stir in ¼ cup milk until blended.

ANISE COOKIES

1/3 cup anise seeds	1 cup light-brown sugar,
3 2/3 cups sifted regular all- purpose flour	packed
1/8 teaspoon baking soda	1 egg, unbeaten
1 cup soft butter or	3 tablespoons light
margarine	molasses
1 cup granulated sugar	1/3 cup undiluted
	evaporated milk

1. With sharp knife, chop anise seeds very fine.
2. Sift flour with baking soda.
3. Cream butter until light and fluffy, gradually adding sugars. Stir in egg, molasses, evaporated milk, and anise seeds; beat well. Blend in flour mixture. Refrigerate covered 1 hour.
4. Shape into rolls 1¼ inches in diameter. Refrigerate at least 12 hours.

To bake:
1. Start heating oven to 375°F.
2. Slice dough ⅛ to ¼ inch thick. Place on ungreased cookie sheets.
3. Bake 9 to 11 minutes, or until done. Makes about 12 dozen.

SO-BIG COOKIES

2 rolls refrigerated slice	Granulated sugar
'n' bake cookies	Nutmeg
(2 favorite flavors)	

1. Start heating oven to 375°F.
2. Slice dough ¼ inch thick. For each cookie, place five slices overlapping in a circle on ungreased cookie sheet, leaving 1-inch hole in center.
3. Bake 10 minutes, or until done.
4. Sprinkle with sugar and nutmeg. Cool 2 or 3 minutes on cookie sheet; remove with large spatula. Makes 1 dozen.

MELTAWAYS

1 cup soft butter or	⅔ cup sifted confectioners'
margarine	sugar
¼ teaspoon salt	2 cups sifted regular all-
½ teaspoon vanilla extract	purpose flour
½ teaspoon almond extract	Colored granulated sugar
	or chopped nuts

1. In large bowl cream butter with salt and vanilla and almond extracts until light and fluffy, gradually adding confectioners' sugar. Blend in flour gradually. Refrigerate 30 minutes, or until dough can be easily handled.
2. Start heating oven to 400°F.
3. Shape dough into rolls about ¾ inch in diameter; cut each roll into ¾-inch lengths. Place, on ends, on ungreased cookie sheet; stamp lightly with flat-bottomed glass, covered with damp cloth. Sprinkle generously with colored granulated sugar or chopped nuts.
4. Bake 10 to 12 minutes, or until done. Makes about 5 dozen.

CHRISTMAS DAISIES
(Pictured on page 47)

1 roll refrigerated slice	White Glaze, below
'n' bake sugar cookies	½ recipe Chocolate Glaze,
Gold dragées	page 51

Make up to 2 weeks before:
1. Start heating oven to 375°F.
2. On floured, cloth-covered surface, roll out half of refrigerated cookie dough very thin. With floured 3-inch daisy cutter, cut out cookies. Place on ungreased cookie sheet. Repeat with other half of dough.
3. Bake 5 to 7 minutes.
4. Cool on wire racks. Meanwhile, make White Glaze. Spread on half of cookies; top each with a dragée.
5. Now make Chocolate Glaze; spread on remaining cookies. Lay white daisies on chocolate cookies with petals alternating as pictured. Store, loosely covered. Makes 3 dozen.

WHITE GLAZE: In bowl, with mixer at medium speed, beat 1 cup confectioners' sugar with about 5 teaspoons water, adding water 1 teaspoon at a time, until of spreading consistency.

RIBBON COOKIES

2½ cups sifted regular all-	1 egg, unbeaten
purpose flour	1 teaspoon vanilla extract
1½ teaspoons double-acting	¼ cup snipped candied
baking powder	cherries
½ teaspoon salt	1 square unsweetened
1 cup soft shortening	chocolate, melted
1¼ cups granulated sugar	2 tablespoons poppy seeds

1. Sift flour with baking powder and salt.
2. Cream shortening until light and fluffy, gradually adding sugar. Stir in egg and vanilla; beat well. Blend in flour mixture.
3. Divide dough into thirds. Add cherries to one third, chocolate to one third, and poppy seeds to remaining third. Into bottom of wax-paper-lined 9-by-5-by-3-inch loaf pan, pack cherry mixture evenly; next, pack in chocolate mixture, then poppy-seed mixture. Cover with wap paper; refrigerate at least 24 hours.

At baking time:
1. Start heating oven to 400°F.
2. Remove dough from pan; cut in half lengthwise, then crosswise into ¼-inch slices. Place on ungreased cookie sheets.
3. Bake 8 to 10 minutes, or until very light brown. Makes 6 to 7 dozen.

CHOCOLATE-SUGAR TWINS
(Pictured on page 8)

1 roll refrigerated slice	*Semisweet-chocolate pieces*
'n' bake sugar cookies	*Granulated sugar*

1. Slice, then bake cookies as label directs.
2. Remove from oven; immediately top half of cookies with 10 to 12 semisweet-chocolate pieces each; lightly sprinkle other half of cookies with sugar.
3. When chocolate pieces have softened, spread evenly over cookies; top each with one of sugared cookies, sandwich fashion. Remove cookies to wire racks to cool. Makes 3½ dozen.

BUTTERSCOTCH PINWHEELS
(Pictured on page 47)

Butterscotch Mixture:	**Chocolate Mixture:**
½ cup soft shortening	*½ cup soft shortening*
1 cup brown sugar, firmly packed	*1 cup granulated sugar*
1 egg, unbeaten	*1 egg, unbeaten*
1 teaspoon vanilla extract	*1 teaspoon vanilla extract*
1½ cups sifted regular all-purpose flour	*1 envelope (1 ounce) no-melt unsweetened chocolate*
½ teaspoon baking soda	*1½ cups sifted regular all-purpose flour*
½ teaspoon salt	*½ teaspoon baking soda*
	½ teaspoon salt

Day before baking:
1. Prepare Butterscotch Mixture: In large bowl, with mixer at medium speed, cream shortening with brown sugar until light and fluffy; beat in egg and vanilla.
2. Onto wax paper sift flour with baking soda and salt; gradually beat into sugar mixture. Divide dough in half; wrap each half in wax paper or saran; refrigerate 1 hour.
3. Prepare Chocolate Mixture: In large bowl, with mixer at medium speed, cream shortening with granulated sugar until light and fluffy. Beat in egg, vanilla, and chocolate.

4. Onto wax paper sift flour with baking soda and salt; gradually beat into sugar mixture. Divide dough in half; wrap each half in wax paper or saran; refrigerate 1 hour.
5. On wax paper, roll half of chocolate dough into 10-by-8-inch rectangle. Lay half of butterscotch dough on top of it and pat it out until it covers chocolate dough. Roll up, jelly-roll fashion; wrap in wax paper or saran. Repeat with other half of both doughs. Refrigerate overnight.
Next day:
1. Start heating oven to 375°F.
2. Slice dough crosswise, ¼ inch thick. Place on greased cookie sheets.
3. Bake 8 to 10 minutes, or until done.
4. Cool; store, in covered container, until served. Makes about 5 dozen.

DARK-RIMMED CHERRY ROUNDS
(Pictured on page 54)

1 roll refrigerated slice	*2 tablespoons cocoa*
'n' bake sugar cookies	*Glacéed cherries*

Make any time up to 2 weeks ahead:
1. Cut roll of dough in half. Roll one half into a 10-inch rope; refrigerate. Into other half work cocoa evenly; then, on lightly-floured surface, roll into 10-by-8-inch rectangle.
2. Lay 10-inch rope across long end of rectangle; roll up, jelly-roll fashion. Pat firmly; wrap in foil; refrigerate overnight.
Next day:
1. Start heating oven to 375°F.
2. Unwrap, then cut dough crosswise into 24 equal slices. Place, about 2 inches apart, on ungreased cookie sheets. Press half a glacéed cherry on each cookie.
3. Bake 8 to 10 minutes.
4. Cool on cookie sheets 5 minutes; remove to wire racks. Store in tightly-covered container. Makes 2 dozen.

CHOCOLATE-TIPPED CRESCENTS

1 roll refrigerated slice	*½ cup semisweet-chocolate pieces*
'n' bake sugar cookies	*Finely-chopped nuts*

1. Start heating oven to 375°F.
2. Cut roll of dough into ¼-inch slices. Mold each slice into crescent. Place, about 2 inches apart, on ungreased cookie sheet.
3. Bake 8 to 10 minutes, or until golden brown.
4. Cool 1 minute; remove to wire rack.
5. Melt chocolate over hot, *not boiling*, water. Spread one end of each cookie with chocolate, then dip into nuts. Makes about 3 dozen.

Homemakers in rural areas still swap cookies at Christmas time, so the idea's surely a natural for city or suburbs. But why not go a step further and swap cookies (or at least favorite cookie recipes) at other times of year. A week or more before the holidays

Old-Time (or before the church bazaar, Fourth-

Cookie of-July picnic, charity bake sale, etc.) each per-

Swap son bakes as many kinds of cookies as her skill — and time — allows. Then you all congregate for a colossal cookie swap. Everyone gets to take home as many cookies as she brought; the trick is to come up with a real assortment—and here is where we come in! The cookies pictured here may give you some pretty good ideas. They are (from left to right): Bow-Tied Holiday Wreaths, Golden Maple Butter Roll-Ups, Double-Walnut Brownie Squares, Iridescent Almond Straws, Christmas Bells, Chocolate Crisps, Pecan-Centered Christmas Stars, Layered Rickrack Rectangles, Lemon-Peel Wheels, Dark-Rimmed Cherry Rounds, Chocolate Orange-Marmalade Bars, Chocolate-Tipped Accordion Strips, and finally we come to Almond-Studded Angel Wings.

CHOCOLATE CRISPS
(Pictured on page 54)

1 6-ounce package (1 cup) semisweet-chocolate pieces	1 teaspoon ginger
1 6-ounce package (1 cup) butterscotch pieces	1¼ cups brown sugar, firmly packed
3 cups sifted regular all-purpose flour	1 cup soft butter or margarine
3 teaspoons double-acting baking powder	1 tablespoon vanilla extract
1 teaspoon salt	2 eggs, unbeaten
1 teaspoon cinnamon	1 cup walnuts, finely chopped

Make any time up to 2 weeks ahead:
1. In small saucepan, over hot, *not boiling,* water, melt chocolate and butterscotch pieces together, stirring occasionally, until smooth.
2. Onto wax paper sift flour with baking powder, salt, cinnamon, and ginger.
3. In large bowl, with mixer at medium speed, beat sugar with butter and vanilla until creamy. Beat in eggs, one at a time, beating well after each addition.
4. Beat in flour, then chocolate-butterscotch mixture until thoroughly blended; stir in nuts. Refrigerate dough until cold.
5. Divide chilled dough into thirds, then shape each third into a roll 2 inches in diameter. Wrap in wax paper or foil; refrigerate overnight.
Next day:
1. Start heating oven to 375°F.
2. Unwrap, then cut each roll into ¼-inch-thick slices. Place on ungreased cookie sheets.
3. Bake 8 to 10 minutes, or until done.
4. Let cool 3 or 4 minutes on cookie sheets; remove to wire racks. Store in loosely-covered container. Makes about 5 dozen.
To freeze: Make and bake cookies as above; freezer-wrap and freeze up to 2 months. To serve, thaw, unwrapped, at room temperature, about 15 minutes.

OATMEAL REFRIGERATOR SLICES

½ cup soft shortening	½ teaspoon salt
½ cup brown sugar, firmly packed	½ teaspoon baking soda
½ cup granulated sugar	1½ cups uncooked quick-cooking rolled oats
1 egg, unbeaten	2 tablespoons milk
1 teaspoon vanilla extract	¼ cup walnuts, finely chopped
¾ cup instant-type flour*	

Make any time up to 2 weeks ahead:
1. In large bowl, with mixer at medium speed, beat shortening with sugars, egg, and vanilla until light and fluffy.
2. On wax paper combine flour with salt and baking soda; then beat into sugar mixture. Stir in oats, milk, and walnuts.
3. Form mixture into a ball, then divide in half. On wax paper, shape each half into a roll 2 inches in diameter; wrap in foil and refrigerate overnight.
Next day:
1. Start heating oven to 350°F.
2. Remove cookie rolls from refrigerator. Slice each, crosswise, into slices ¼ inch thick. Place on ungreased cookie sheets.
3. Bake 10 to 12 minutes, or until done.
4. Cool on wire racks; store in loosely-covered container. Makes about 25.
To freeze: Make cookies as above. Freezer-wrap and freeze up to 2 months. To serve, thaw, unwrapped, at room temperature about 15 minutes.
*Do not sift this flour.

OATMEAL LOLLIPOPS

1 roll refrigerated slice 'n' bake oatmeal cookies	Semisweet-chocolate pieces
	Gumdrops
	Cinnamon candies
Frosting for "glue"	Yellow flaked coconut

1. Start heating oven to 375°F.
2. Shape dough into 16 balls. Place on ungreased cookie sheet. Flatten each with bottom of glass dipped in flour. Insert wooden skewer in each.
3. Bake 10 minutes.
4. Cool. With frosting, attach semisweet-chocolate pieces for eyes, bit of gumdrop for nose, cinnamon candies for mouth, and flaked coconut for hair. Makes 16 lollipops.

COCONUT-OATMEAL REFRIGERATOR COOKIES

1½ cups sifted regular all-purpose flour	1 cup granulated sugar
1 teaspoon baking soda	2 eggs, unbeaten
1 teaspoon salt	3 cups uncooked quick-cooking rolled oats
1 cup soft shortening (part butter)	½ cup chopped pecans
1 cup brown sugar, packed	1½ cups flaked coconut

1. Sift flour with baking soda and salt.
2. Cream shortening until light and fluffy, gradually

adding sugars. Add eggs; beat well. Blend in flour mixture, then rolled oats gradually. Stir in pecans and coconut.

3. Shape dough into 3 rolls, 2 inches in diameter; wrap each in wax paper. Refrigerate at least 24 hours.

To bake:

1. Start heating oven to 375°F.
2. Slice dough ⅛ to ¼ inch thick. Place on ungreased cookie sheets.
3. Bake 10 minutes, or until done. Makes 6 dozen.

ORANGE-COCONUT BARS

1 roll refrigerated slice
  'n' bake coconut cookies
1 cup chopped walnuts
1 cup flaked coconut

2 tablespoons grated
  orange peel
1 tablespoon orange juice

1. Start heating oven to 375°F.
2. Slice dough about ¾-inch thick; then quarter each slice. Press quarters, side by side, into ungreased 13-by-9-by-2-inch pan.
3. Combine walnuts, coconut, orange peel and juice; lightly press into dough.
4. Bake 20 to 25 minutes, or until golden brown.
5. Cool; cut into bars. Makes about 3 dozen.

PEANUT-BUTTER SPARKLERS

1 roll refrigerated slice
  'n' bake peanut-butter
  cookies
Granulated sugar

Semisweet-chocolate
  pieces and/or
  miniature marshmallows

1. Start heating oven to 375°F.
2. Slice dough as label directs. Cut each slice in half; roll into a ball, then roll in sugar. Place on ungreased cookie sheet.
3. Bake 6 to 8 minutes, or until light brown.
4. Now, into each ball, press lightly 1 or more chocolate pieces or marshmallows. Return to oven; bake 2 minutes longer.
5. Cool 1 minute; remove to wire racks. Makes 3 dozen.

PECAN CRISPS

1 cup soft butter or
  margarine
⅛ teaspoon salt
½ cup sifted confectioners'
  sugar
2 teaspoons vanilla extract

2 cups finely-chopped
  pecans
1½ cups sifted regular all-
  purpose flour
Confectioners' sugar

1. Start heating oven to 325°F.
2. Cream butter with salt until light and fluffy, gradually adding ½ cup sugar. Blend in vanilla, pecans, then flour.

3. On lightly-floured surface, shape portions of dough into rolls, about ½ inch in diameter. Slice into 1½-inch pieces. Place, about 2 inches apart, on ungreased cookie sheets.
4. Bake 15 to 20 minutes.
5. While cookies are still warm, roll them in confectioners' sugar. Makes about 6 dozen.

PECAN-CENTERED CHRISTMAS STARS
(Pictured on page 54)

1 roll refrigerated slice
  'n' bake sugar cookies
Rum Butter Cream, page 17
Pecan halves

½ cup semisweet-
  chocolate pieces
Ground pecans

Make any time up to 2 weeks ahead:

1. Start heating oven to 375°F.
2. On floured, cloth-covered surface, roll out dough very thin. Cut, with floured 4-inch star-shaped cutter, into 36 stars. Place on ungreased cookie sheets.
3. Bake about 5 minutes, or until golden.
4. Cool on wire racks; store loosely-covered.

Day before or early on day:

1. Spread 18 stars with Rum Butter Cream; top with rest of stars. With bit of butter cream, center pecan half on each.
2. Melt chocolate pieces over hot, *not boiling*, water; glaze points of each star; top some with ground pecans. Cool until chocolate hardens; refrigerate, covered, until ready to serve. Makes 18.

WALNUT FREEZER ROLL

1 cup butter or margarine
2 cups brown sugar, packed
2 eggs, unbeaten
1 teaspoon vanilla extract
3 cups sifted regular all-
  purpose flour

3 teaspoons double-acting
  baking powder
½ teaspoon salt
1½ cups coarsely-chopped
  walnuts

Make, then freeze, as follows:

1. With mixer at medium speed beat butter with sugar until light and fluffy. Beat in eggs and vanilla.
2. Sift flour with baking powder and salt; beat into butter mixture. Stir in walnuts. Wrap in foil; refrigerate several hours, or until firm.
3. Divide dough in half; shape into 2 long rolls about 2 inches in diameter; freezer-wrap, then freeze.

To bake:

1. Start heating oven to 375°F.
2. Unwrap cookie dough; slice off as many cookies as desired, about ⅛ to ¼ inch thick. Rewrap the unused portion and return to freezer. Place slices on greased cookie sheet.
3. Bake about 8 minutes, or until light brown.
4. Cool on wire racks. Makes about 7 dozen.

PEPPERMINT FLUFFS
(Pictured on page 12)

2 egg whites, unbeaten
½ cup granulated sugar
⅛ teaspoon peppermint
  extract

Green food color
1 roll refrigerated slice
  'n' bake sugar cookies
Green crystal sugar

Make early on day:
1. Start heating oven to 325°F.
2. In medium bowl, with mixer at high speed, beat egg whites until foamy; then gradually beat in sugar, beating well after each addition. Continue beating until stiff peaks form when beater is raised. Fold in peppermint extract and few drops green food color, then set this meringue mixture aside.
3. Slice roll of dough ⅛ inch thick. Place slices, about 2 inches apart, on ungreased cookie sheets. With some of meringue in decorating bag with tube number 6 in place, press large rosette onto top of each cookie; sprinkle with green crystal sugar.
4. Bake about 12 minutes, or until lightly browned.
5. Cool slightly on cookie sheets; remove to wire racks. Makes about 50.

Deep-Fried Cookies

Scandinavian in origin, these delicate, pastry-like cookies are popular the world around. They are just what the name implies—deep-fried in salad oil or shortening, then dusted with confectioners' sugar for an intriguing not-too-sweet, melt-in-the-mouth flavor sensation.

FRIDA'S ROSETTES

Salad oil or shortening
  for deep-fat frying
2 eggs, unbeaten
1 tablespoon granulated
  sugar
⅛ teaspoon salt

1 cup milk
1 cup sifted regular all-
  purpose flour
1 teaspoon vanilla extract
Confectioners' sugar

Make several days ahead, or early on day:
1. In deep saucepan or deep-fat fryer, heat 2 to 3 inches of salad oil to 365°F. on deep-fat-frying thermometer.
2. Meanwhile, in medium bowl, with fork, slightly beat eggs with granulated sugar and salt. Add milk, flour, and vanilla; then, with hand beater, beat just until smooth.
3. In hot oil, heat rosette iron* for 3 *minutes.* Then, at once, dip it in batter only to within ¼ inch to top of iron, and hold it there a few seconds; then dip again. (Be sure not to dip entire iron into batter or rosette will be difficult to remove when done.)
4. Immediately lower iron into hot oil, immersing it *completely.* Fry about 1 minute, or until rosette is a delicate brown.
5. Then lift iron out of oil; with four-tined fork, carefully loosen rosette; remove and let drain on paper towel.
6. Immediately dip iron in batter again, and fry as above. Repeat until all batter is used.
7. Store in tightly-covered container. Just before serving, sprinkle with confectioners' sugar. Makes about 30.
*Rosette irons can be purchased in a housewares department.

RABBIT'S EARS
(Fattigman)

4 cups sifted regular
  all-purpose flour
⅓ cup granulated sugar
½ cup butter or margarine
3 eggs, slightly beaten
1 teaspoon cardamom

1 tablespoon cognac
¼ cup heavy cream
Salad oil or shortening
  for deep-fat frying
Confectioners' sugar

Make day before, or several days ahead:
1. Sift flour with granulated sugar.
2. In large bowl, with mixer at medium speed, beat butter until light and fluffy. Gradually beat in flour mixture. Then add eggs, cardamom, cognac, and cream, beating until thoroughly blended.
3. Wrap dough in foil, wax paper, or saran; refrigerate until well chilled.
4. Divide chilled dough into fourths. On lightly-floured surface, roll out one-fourth of dough *paper thin* (refrigerate remainder). Cut into strips 1½-inches wide; cut each strip into 4- to 5-inch pieces. Make a 1-inch slash along lengthwise center of each piece. Now pull one end of piece all the way through this slash. Repeat with rest of dough.
5. In deep saucepan or deep-fat fryer, heat 2 inches of salad oil to 380°F. on deep-fat-frying thermometer.
6. Drop in pieces, a few at a time. Fry until golden on both sides, turning once.
7. Remove from oil; drain on paper towels. When cool, sprinkle with confectioners 'sugar. Store in tightly-covered container. Makes about 80.

No-Bake Cookies

These quick-to-fix, fun-to-mix cookies are perfect for hot summer days when you don't want to turn on the oven, but they're equally great for holiday gift-giving time. No-bake cookies take many forms — dropped, molded, sliced — and many flavors. Try them all!

QUICK MACAROONS
(Pictured on page 8)

⅓ cup undiluted evaporated milk	½ teaspoon vanilla extract
2 tablespoons butter or margarine	1 cup flaked coconut
¾ cup granulated sugar	½ cup coarsely-broken pecans
	1½ cups cornflakes

1. In large saucepan combine evaporated milk, butter, and sugar. Cook, stirring constantly, until mixture comes to full rolling boil. Then lower heat and continue to boil, stirring constantly, for 2 minutes. Remove from heat.
2. Quickly stir in vanilla, coconut, pecans, and cornflakes, making sure all pieces are well coated with milk mixture.
3. Now, using two teaspoons, quickly drop mixture in mounds, onto wax-paper-lined cookie sheet. Refrigerate until firm. Makes about 12.

CHOCOLATE BITS
(Pictured on page 47)

1 6-ounce package semi-sweet-chocolate pieces	1 6½-ounce package creamy-white-frosting mix
3 tablespoons white corn syrup	Red food color
1 tablespoon water	Flaked coconut or minced walnuts
1 cup blanched almonds, finely chopped	Cinnamon candies

Make any time up to 1 week ahead:
1. In double boiler, over hot, *not boiling*, water, combine chocolate pieces with corn syrup and water; heat until chocolate melts and mixture is smooth, stirring occasionally. Remove from water.

2. Stir in almonds. Then drop, by scant half teaspoonfuls onto wax-paper-lined cookie sheets. Refrigerate until firm.
3. Meanwhile, make up frosting as label directs; with food color tint a delicate pink. Use to spread on tops of chilled cookies. Let dry a bit, then dip each cookie in coconut or walnuts; top each with a cinnamon candy. Refrigerate until served. Makes about 75.

TING-A-LINGS
(Pictured on page 47)

1 6-ounce package semisweet-chocolate pieces	1 3-ounce can chow-mein noodles
½ cup canned salted peanuts	Candied cherries

Make several days ahead:
1. In double boiler, over hot, *not boiling*, water, melt chocolate pieces; stir in peanuts and noodles until they are well coated with chocolate.
2. Drop, by heaping teaspoonfuls, onto wax-paper-lined cookie sheet. Top each with a quartered candied cherry. Refrigerate until served. If they soften when served, refrigerate again until firm. Makes about 3 dozen.

CHOCOLATE-CORNFLAKE CLUSTERS
(Pictured on page 12)

1 6-ounce package semi-sweet-chocolate pieces	2 cups crisp ready-to-eat cereal
3 tablespoons white corn syrup	Cinnamon candies (optional)
1 tablespoon water	Candied citron, finely chopped (optional)

Make a few days ahead:
1. In double boiler, over hot, *not boiling* water, melt chocolate pieces with corn syrup and water; stir to blend. Remove from water.
2. Add cereal; stir until well coated. Drop by rounded teaspoonfuls onto foil-covered cookie sheets. Decorate with cinnamon candies and citron.
3. Refrigerate until firm. Makes about 2½ dozen.
To vary: Make as above, but substitute for the cereal one of the following—
½ cup chopped mixed preserved fruit and ½ cup chopped walnuts
1 cup flaked coconut and ½ cup chopped candied cherries
1 cup miniature marshmallows and 1 cup salted peanuts
2 cups cornflakes, ½ cup chopped dates, and ½ cup chopped pecans
2 cups raisins
1 3-ounce can (2 cups) chow-mein noodles and 1 cup chopped dates

60

Brandy Balls

BRANDY BALLS
(Pictured opposite)

2 7¼-ounce packages
 vanilla wafers, rolled
 into fine crumbs
½ cup liquid honey
⅓ cup brandy

⅓ cup light rum
1 pound shelled walnuts,
 finely ground
Granulated sugar

Make up to a week ahead:
1. In bowl mix together crumbs, honey, brandy, rum, and walnuts.
2. Shape into bite-size balls; roll in granulated sugar. Wrap each ball in saran. The flavor improves with holding! Makes about 5 dozen.

NO-BAKE COOKIE BALLS

1 6-ounce package semi-
 sweet-chocolate pieces
 (1 cup)
3 tablespoons white corn
 syrup
2 teaspoons instant coffee
 powder
⅓ cup hot water

3 cups sifted confectioners'
 sugar
1 cup chopped walnuts
About 3 dozen packaged
 vanilla wafers, finely
 crushed (1¾ cups)
Confectioners' sugar

1. In double boiler, over hot, *not boiling,* water, melt chocolate pieces; remove from heat.
2. Stir in corn syrup, coffee dissolved in hot water, 3 cups sugar, walnuts, and crumbs.
3. Shape into 1-inch balls; roll in confectioners' sugar. Store in covered container a day or so to ripen. Makes about 5 dozen.

CHOCO-ORANGE BALLS: Substitute ⅓ cup orange juice for coffee and hot water.

SURPRISE BALLS (Pictured on page 8): Cut 1 large nutted candy bar into 4 dozen small pieces. Around each piece mold some of chocolate mixture into 1-inch ball; complete as directed.

HONEY CANDY BITES

½ cup butter or margarine
2 tablespoons milk
1 cup instant-type flour*
¾ cup liquid honey
¼ teaspoon salt

1 teaspoon vanilla extract
1½ cups flaked coconut
2 cups crisp rice cereal
½ cup flaked coconut

Make several days ahead:
1. In medium saucepan melt butter; stir in milk, flour, honey, and salt. Cook over medium heat, stirring constantly, until mixture leaves sides of pan and forms a ball; remove from heat.
2. Stir in vanilla, 1½ cups coconut, and cereal.
3. Shape into 1-inch balls; roll in ½ cup coconut. Refrigerate until served. Makes about 3 dozen.
*Do not sift this flour.

COCONUT-DATE PORCUPINES

¾ cup granulated sugar
1 cup snipped pitted dates
2 eggs, well beaten
1 teaspoon vanilla extract
1 cup chopped walnuts

1 cup cornflakes
1 cup sugar-coated toasted
 rice cereal
1½ cups flaked coconut

1. In skillet blend sugar with dates and eggs. Cook over medium heat, stirring constantly, until mixture pulls away from sides of pan (about 5 minutes); remove from heat.
2. Stir in vanilla and walnuts; then carefully stir in cereals. Cool slightly.
3. With hands, moistened with cold water, shape mixture into small mounds; roll each in coconut. Refrigerate until served. Makes 2 dozen.
Note: If desired, omit coconut and dip each in melted semisweet chocolate.

WALNUT BOURBON BALLS

About 5 dozen packaged
 vanilla wafers, finely
 crushed (2½ cups)
2 tablespoons cocoa
1 cup sifted confectioners'
 sugar

1 cup finely-chopped
 walnuts, or walnuts
 and flaked coconut
3 tablespoons corn syrup
¼ cup bourbon
Confectioners' sugar

1. Mix together well crumbs, cocoa, 1 cup sugar, and walnuts. Add corn syrup and bourbon; mix well.
2. Shape into 1-inch balls; roll in confectioners' sugar. Store in covered container a day or so to ripen; these keep very well. Makes 3½ dozen.

CHOCOLATE-BUTTERSCOTCH BARS
(Pictured on page 12)

2 6-ounce packages
 butterscotch pieces
2 tablespoons shortening
1 cup chopped walnuts
1½ cups miniature
 marshmallows

2 6-ounce packages
 semisweet-chocolate
 pieces
About 20 walnut halves
 (optional)

Make several days before, if desired, or on day:
1. In double boiler, over hot, *not boiling,* water, melt butterscotch pieces with 1 tablespoon shortening. Remove from heat; stir in chopped walnuts. Spread in well-greased 8-by-8-by-2-inch pan.
2. Arrange marshmallows evenly over butterscotch layer, gently pressing into surface.
3. In same double boiler, over hot, *not boiling,* water, melt chocolate pieces with 1 tablespoon shortening. Spread chocolate mixture evenly over marshmallow layer; lay walnut halves in soft chocolate.
4. Cool, then refrigerate until ready to serve. Cut into 48 bars.

Sugarbush-Tree Lollipops

SUGARBUSH-TREE LOLLIPOPS
(Pictured above)

6 cups puffed rice	Green food color
¼ cup butter or margarine	Assorted tubes decorating
32 large marshmallows	gels*
2 tablespoons dark corn	Candy dots
syrup	Chocolate sprinkles
	Colored sugars

Make about 1 week ahead:
1. Start heating oven to 400°F.
2. In shallow baking pan, heat puffed rice in oven for 5 minutes; turn into large greased bowl.
3. In double boiler, over hot water, melt butter with marshmallows, stirring occasionally. Stir in corn syrup, then beat with spoon until smooth. Pour over hot puffed rice, tossing rice with fork until all is well coated.
4. Now, if desired, color wooden skewers by brushing each with a few drops green food color dissolved in 3 tablespoons water. Grease 1 or more treelike, triangular-shaped cookie cutters. Place on wax paper, on flat surface, sharp edges down.
5. Pack each cookie cutter with puffed rice mixture; gently push mixture out onto wax paper; insert a wooden skewer in each. Repeat, greasing cookie cutter each time, until 15 trees are made.
6. Decorate trees with decorating gels, candy dots, sprinkles, or colored sugars, as pictured. Tie bow of gold cord on each skewer. Then arrange trees side by side in baking pan; cover with saran until needed. Makes 15 4-by-3-inch tree lollipops.
*Available from Timely Brands, Heublein, East Hampton, Massachusetts.

NO-COOK CHOCOLATE COOKIES

¼ cup butter or	Dash salt
margarine, melted	1 cup coarsely-chopped
½ cup white corn syrup	nuts
⅔ cup cocoa	⅔ cup flaked coconut
1 cup sifted confectioners'	6 ounces candy-coated
sugar	puffed wheat (4½ cups)

1. In large bowl blend butter with corn syrup, cocoa, sugar, and salt. Add nuts, coconut, and cereal; with fork, stir mixture until cereal is well coated.
2. Pack mixture firmly into greased 13-by-9-by-2-inch pan. Refrigerate several hours, or until firm. Cut into squares. Makes 3 to 4 dozen.

CRUNCHY SKILLET COOKIES

2 tablespoons butter or	2 eggs, well beaten
margarine	3 cups crisp rice cereal
1 cup finely-snipped	½ cup chopped walnuts
pitted dates	Confectioners' sugar
1 cup granulated sugar	

Make several days ahead or on day:
1. In 10-inch skillet melt butter. Add dates and granulated sugar; blend well. Now, while stirring, add eggs. Cook over low heat, stirring constantly, allowing mixture to bubble softly, until it forms a soft ball when a little is dropped into a glass of cold water—5 or 6 minutes. Remove from heat.
2. Cool slightly; then stir in cereal and nuts, blending well. Turn out onto large sheet of wax paper that has been lightly sprinkled with confectioners' sugar. Roll to coat well on all sides.

3. Divide mixture into thirds; shape each third into a roll 5 inches long and 1½ to 2 inches in diameter. Wrap each in wax paper. Refrigerate.

4. When needed, slice each cookie roll into ¼-inch-thick slices. Makes about 60.

TRIANGLES
(Pictured on page 47)

½ cup butter or margarine
2 eggs, well beaten
1 cup granulated sugar
1 10-ounce package pitted dates, snipped into bits (1½ cups)
½ cup instant-type flour*

½ teaspoon salt
1 teaspoon vanilla extract
1 cup walnuts, finely chopped
2½ cups crisp rice cereal
Red-colored sugar

Make several days ahead:

1. In large saucepan melt butter; then stirring constantly, add eggs and granulated sugar; mix, with a spoon, until very thoroughly blended.

2. Stir in dates; cook 5 minutes, stirring constantly. Gradually stir in flour. Cook, stirring constantly, until thick—2 to 3 minutes. Remove from heat. Stir in salt, vanilla, nuts, and cereal.

3. Divide mixture in half; on wax paper shape each half into a roll 12-inches long. Flatten sides of rolls to form triangular shapes; then pat colored sugar into sides of each. Refrigerate for at least 24 hours.

4. Cut each roll into 24 crosswise slices; refrigerate until served. Makes about 48.

*Do not sift this flour.

....

Cookies for Dieters

....

No need to starve your sweet tooth just because you are counting calories or watching your sugar —here are cookies that will satisfy that craving.

SNOWFLAKES
(low calorie)

2 egg whites, unbeaten
¼ teaspoon salt
⅓ cup granulated sugar

¾ teaspoon almond extract
½ cup flaked coconut

1. Start heating oven to 250°F.

2. With mixer or hand beater, beat egg whites and salt until soft peaks are formed. Add sugar, a tablespoonful at a time, beating until mixture is very stiff. Gently fold in almond extract and coconut.

3. Drop, by spoonfuls, onto very-well-greased cookie sheet.

4. Bake 45 minutes; turn off heat and keep cookies in oven until they are cool and crisp.

5. Remove from oven; store in tightly-covered container until served. Makes 1½ dozen. (*25 calories per cookie*)

LEMON SNAP COOKIES
(low calorie)

½ cup butter or margarine
¾ cup granulated sugar
1 egg, unbeaten
1½ teaspoons grated lemon peel
2 tablespoons lemon juice

2¼ cups sifted regular all-purpose flour
½ teaspoon double-acting baking powder
¼ teaspoon salt

1. In medium bowl cream together butter with sugar until light and fluffy; beat in egg, lemon peel and lemon juice.

2. Sift flour with baking powder and salt. Add gradually to sugar mixture; mix until smooth. Refrigerate until firm—1 to 2 hours.

3. Start heating oven to 400°F.

4. On well-floured surface, roll out dough to ⅛-inch thickness. With 2-inch round or favorite cookie cutter, cut out cookies. Place on lightly-greased cookie sheets.

5. Bake 6 to 8 minutes, or until edges are golden brown. Makes about 6 or 7 dozen. (*30 calories per cookie*)

BROWNIES
(diabetic)

½ cup butter or margarine
Nonnutritive sweetener equivalent to 1¼ cups sugar (if tablets are used, pulverize them to fine powder)
2 squares unsweetened chocolate, melted

2 eggs, unbeaten
½ teaspoon vanilla extract
¾ cup sifted regular all-purpose flour
1 teaspoon double-acting baking powder
½ cup chopped walnuts

1. Start heating oven to 350°F.

2. In large bowl cream butter with nonnutritive sweetener until light and fluffy; add chocolate; beat until smooth. Beat in eggs and vanilla. Add flour, baking powder, and walnuts; beat until smooth.

3. Spread batter in greased 8-by-8-by-2-inch pan.

4. Bake 30 minutes, or until surface of brownies is shiny.

5. Cool in pan; cut into 16 squares. (*100 calories and ½ bread and 2 fat exchanges per square*)

Index